Haunted
Hotels

Haunted Hotels

*A Guide to
American and Canadian Inns
and Their Ghosts*

ROBIN MEAD

Illustrated by Pamela Wright

RUTLEDGE HILL PRESS

Nashville, Tennessee

Published in Nashville, Tennessee, by Rutledge Hill Press, Inc.
211 Seventh Avenue North, Nashville, Tennessee 37219.

Distributed in Canada by H. B. Fenn & Company, Ltd.,
34 Nixon Road, Bolton, Ontario L7E 1W2.

Distributed in the United Kingdom by Verulam Publishing, Ltd.,
152a Park Street Lane, Park Street, St. Albans, Hertfordshire AL2 2AU

Designed by Bruce Gore / Gore Studio, Inc.

Library of Congress Cataloging-in-Publication Data

Mead, Robin.
    Haunted hotels : a guide to American and Canadian inns and
their ghosts / Robin Mead.
        p.   cm.
    ISBN 1-55853-369-9
        1. Haunted hotels—United States—Guidebooks.   2. Haunted
hotels—Canada—Guidebooks.   3. Ghosts—United States.
    4. Ghost—Canada.
    I. Title.
    BF1474.5.M43   1995
    133.1'22—dc20   95-25168
                                                                CIP

Printed in the United States of America

2 3 4 5 6 7 8 9   99 98 97 96

CONTENTS

ACKNOWLEDGMENTS

THIS BOOK could not have been written without the advice, assistance, and information provided by various organizations. They include that wonderfully supportive duo, the U.S. Travel and Tourism Administration, and the Travel Industry Association of America; many state tourist boards (especially California, Maine, Maryland, and Wyoming); the National Trust for Historic Preservation; Ritz-Carlton Hotels; and Best Western.

The author also thanks the following individuals for their help and ideas, much of it provided above and beyond the call of duty: William Armistead, Eric and Ruth Bailey, Michael Cerletti, Mary Kay Cline, David Collins, Cammie Conlon, Anita Cotter, Hugh DeSamper, Charlotte Fenn, Mary Foley Billingsley, Penny Golding, Sarah Graham Mann, Elisabeth Lewis-Jones, Robin Maydeck, Polly Mead, Bruce Morgan, Anne North, Fred Sater, Martha Steger, and Kenneth Westcott-Jones.

Special thanks go to Pamela Wright, who did the wonderful drawings in this book, and to Jacqui Young who typed the manuscript.

INTRODUCTION

THIS IS not a book for or from the lunatic fringe. It is, first and foremost, a hotel guide. In it you will find described, in some detail, a selection of the best places to stay in North America.

The hotels, guesthouses, inns, and bed-and-breakfasts featured here vary enormously in size, price, and ambiance. They include some of the grandest and best-known establishments in the United States and Canada. Also included is a variety of more modest hotels, some interesting inns, and a hand-picked selection of bed-and-breakfast accommodations.

All the properties listed in *Haunted Hotels* have two things in common. First, they offer good value as wonderful destinations for a weekend break, or perhaps a longer vacation. Second, visitors to these properties might discover that some of their fellow guests are not of the tangible variety.

Do you believe in ghosts? You have every opportunity to, because North America has a strong tradition of hauntings. The best-known stories come from spiritual places such as the ancient Indian hunting grounds of the Midwest, colonial New England, the antebellum plantation homes of the Deep South (where slavery and a sybaritic lifestyle once existed side by side), and from the Civil War battlefields.

But as this book demonstrates, they are also to be found in the once-Wild West, on the island paradise of Hawaii, high in the Canadian Rockies, amid the beaches of Florida, and even on the star-studded streets of Hollywood. In fact, in terms of haunted places to stay, California has a better choice than any other of America's fifty states or Canada's twelve provinces and territories.

There's a worldwide population of ghosts. Their habitat ranges from Australia's aboriginal lands to the snowy summits of Tibet, and from Scotland's gaunt castles to the lonely villages amid the mountains on the Greek island of Crete.

But North American ghosts have become world-renowned tourist attractions in their own right. Just look at the popularity of the Winchester Mystery House in San Jose, California—an odd building with an even stranger history and certainly one of the country's eeriest places. Along with all the other information needed for this book came thick files of material detailing "ghost walks" and even longer tours throughout the United States. One tempting brochure offers this tantalizing invitation:

> Meet on Main Street at 8:00 P.M. on Saturday night and join a lantern-led ghost tour through New Hope, Pennsylvania. See the historic inn where Aaron Barr stares with sightless eyes.

Unfortunately, no other clue is offered as to the exact whereabouts of this inn or Mr. Barr's identity.

Other regions likewise offer such supernatural sensations. Pennsylvania's Bucks County and Tennessee's Historic Rugby offer spooky strolls. In Washington, D.C., a local historian leads weekend walks right by the White House. It includes a segment where "the Curse of Lafayette Square is expounded." Mississippi boasts so many ghosts that officials even offer week-long tour itineraries available for tour operators and group travel organizers. Tongue in cheek, organizers refer to these trips as "spirited adventures."

Many of North America's most atmospheric and historic places, while rich in legend, folklore, and spooky stories, don't actually boast a haunted hotel. Colonial Williamsburg in Virginia, for example, is one such town, despite the fact that a particularly gruesome murder took place in the historic area's Chiswell-Bucktrout Tavern, still one of Colonial Williamsburg's overnight accommodations. Quebec City, the oldest city in Canada, is another. At the spectacular Montmorency Falls, only nine miles from downtown, tens of thousands of people have witnessed the phenomenon of "La Dame Blanche" (the White Lady)—the figure of a girl who drowned in the falls and appears in the mist thrown up by the spray. Still, there is no haunted hotel in town.

Americans, especially tourists, are fascinated with ghosts. One of the first questions asked by guests arriving at a hotel or inn reeking of unique atmosphere is, "Do you have a ghost?" In *Haunted Hotels*, you will find a selection of those who answer yes. Stories told by these hoteliers, innkeepers, and hosts are extraordinarily varied. Some are sad. Some are puzzling. A few are even funny. The spirit world is not without its sense of humor.

On the other hand, the ghosts profiled here aren't particularly frightening. There are no Freddie Kruegers or poltergeists prone to violence. There are no screaming banshees or chain-rattling ghouls to disturb your slumbers. Nevertheless, some haunted hotels, fearful that a ghost story might put off some prospective customers, have asked not to be included here.

Other properties make a positive promotion of their ghosts. The fifty-five-bedroom Colonial Inn in Concord, Massachusetts, makes no secret that Room 24 is haunted—and has found it to be a valuable marketing tool. An official report issued four years ago notes that Room 24 "enjoys practically continuous booking since word got out about its haunting." The National Trust for Historic Preservation also makes no secret of the fact that seven of its member hotels are haunted—all of them household names. (For a copy of the Historic Hotels of America membership directory, send three dollars to Historic Hotels of America, National Trust for Historic Preservation, 1785 Massachusetts Avenue NW, Washington, D.C. 20036.) Historic Hotels of America also operates its own central bookings service (telephone 800-678-8946).

In California, a number of hotels are so proud of their ghosts, they're treated like film stars. Come to think of it, a couple of the ghosts *are* film stars. Most of the listed hotels, guesthouses, inns, and bed-and-breakfasts, however, handle their resident ghost(s) much as they would any other long-term resident—with a sort of cheery familiarity tempered with a modicum of respect.

Although there are many schemes commonly used to rate hotels and their respective perks, no one has dreamed up an acceptable means for grading the degree of comfort and service that a haunted property offers its guests. But if such a scheme is invented, all the accommodations profiled in this book probably would get the highest possible grade. The author's personal experience and on-the-spot investigation suggest that every one of them is very warm and welcoming.

Even if you don't hear or see a ghost at one of these places, you will at least have a pleasant stay. Perhaps you will even succeed where I failed. Although I found any number of properties with a distinctly odd atmosphere, observed a few mysterious shadows here and there, and heard some very strange nocturnal noises, I didn't actually spot a spook.

Or did I? On the beautiful Guenoc Winery in California stands the Lillie Langtry House—once the holiday home of the British actress reputed to have been the mistress of the Prince of Wales (later King Edward VII). Although it has a couple of guest rooms, the Lillie Langtry House is not normally open to visitors unless they are the guests of the winery. During a swing through northern California, however, I was invited to dinner with the winery's owner, Orville Magoon. After dinner I was offered a bed in the otherwise empty Lillie Langtry House. To make my lonely vigil even spookier, I was put in the room formerly occupied by "the Jersey Lily" herself. It is a lovely room, in a lovely old house. But I certainly felt (although I did not see) a "presence" in the room during the night. And if, in the dawn, the tapping I heard on my door can be attributed to the peculiar sense of humor possessed by my guide from the state office of tourism . . . well, that's all part of the fun of a "weekend haunt."

I have more strange, and rather less easily explained, experiences to report from Louisiana—as you will discover when you browse through this book. And whether you just want to read about America's haunted accommodations, or you want to go and enjoy them for yourself, happy ghost-hunting!

Robin Mead

Haunted Hotels

AUTHOR'S NOTE:

Nothing dates a book faster than the changing prices charged by hotels, inns, and B&Bs for meals and accommodation. Most of these change annually. So, for ease of reference, the price range of each property in this book is described only as "Inexpensive," "Moderate," or "Expensive." As a rough guide, and based upon Summer 1996 room tariffs, these may be divided as follows:

Inexpensive: Up to about $100 per night
Moderate: Around $100 to $200 per night
Expensive: More than $200 per night

ALABAMA

GRACE HALL

Selma, Alabama

GRACE HALL is a beautifully restored antebellum mansion, built in 1857 by Henry Ware and occupied for the next 110 years by—in turn—the Evans, Baker, and Jones families.

Architecturally, the house mixes elements of the older neoclassicism with the newer Victorian trends. It is on the *National Register of Historic Places*, and the restoration has been certified by the Department of the Interior. It is now run as a bed-and-breakfast, although it is also available for tours, parties, business, and social events, and meals for groups of ten or more. Tours are by appointment.

There are six guest bedrooms, all of them backing onto a brightly painted and flower-filled courtyard. The furnishings are on a grand scale: four-poster beds, silk coverlets, thick lace curtains, heavy mahogany furniture, and period wallpaper. The rooms have private baths.

The public areas are especially eye-catching. The hall is magnificent. Colored glass panels surround the front door and, along with the chandelier, are reflected in a huge mirror and in the gleaming wooden floor. There are double parlors, both extremely elegant and filled with fine furniture. Guest rates include morning coffee, a full breakfast, and a guided tour of the mansion and its treasures.

Historic Selma, which stands high above the Alabama River near Montgomery, was the scene of frequent bombardments during the Civil War. But despite the enormous destruction, sufficient architecturally attractive homes survived to give the town an aura of antebellum life. Sturdivant Hall, a restored neoclassical building dating from

1852, was designed by a relative of Robert E. Lee and is worth seeing. Swimming, fishing, and hiking are popular in wooded Valley Creek State Park, seventeen miles from Selma.

THE GHOST at Grace Hall is "Miz Eliza," who lived in the house in the latter part of the nineteenth century. Miz Eliza's dog, her aunt, Miss Evans—or "Old Miss" as she was known to her friends—and a former black servant named Pappy King have also been seen at Grace Hall in recent years. There could even be a couple more ghosts.

Owners Coy and Joey Dillon say that Miz Eliza was first sighted at Grace Hall in the summer of 1982, while the house was being restored. Coy explains: "One hot summer evening at about 7:00 P.M., we closed up Grace Hall to go to another residence that we had leased while the restoration was in progress, and we decided to take some pictures of the work that day. One negative remained on the roll so, as we left, we took a picture of the exterior. Much to our amazement, when developed, the photo showed a figure standing in the Palladian window."

The Dillons' initial surprise gave way to common sense, and they dismissed the figure in the window as a trick of the light. But when the restoration work was complete and the house was once again open to guests, three small children who were staying there inquired about "the beautiful lady with the long white gown" they had seen on the upper stairway. The lady, they added, had been accompanied by a small black dog. Former owner Grace Jones, after whom the house is named, was consulted and decided the apparition was the ghost of her mother, Miz Eliza, accompanied by her faithful pet, Barney Doolittle, a little black dog that never left her side in life and appeared to be accompanying her still.

"Ever since that second sighting, Miz Eliza has been a regular, most often appearing when young ladies or small children are in the house," Coy Dillon says. As a mother with four daughters of her own, Miz Eliza might be expected to delight in the company of youngsters. But she gave a doctor's bride a rude awakening when she appeared beside the bed one night, and the bridegroom ended up having to sedate his frightened wife.

In another sighting, a young lady guest was having trouble sleeping after the death of her twin brother. After getting out of bed in the middle of the night to sit on the porch, she saw a white-haired, elderly lady standing on the other side of a fountain in the garden. The guest was not surprised by this and imagined she was watching someone else who couldn't sleep. But when she struck her cigarette lighter, the figure of the old lady simply vanished. In this instance, the apparition was accompanied by a second figure—an elderly black man. Could the strange couple have been Old Miss and her retainer Pappy King, whom she had brought with her when she first came to Grace Hall?

The Dillons are anxious to point out that, until recently, they themselves had not seen any of their ghosts, although they had sensed their presence on many occasions. They add that Miz Eliza "appears" rather than "haunts." She is a very happy spirit who causes them no worry. There is no particularly haunted room, or spot, in the inn—but in general, Miz Eliza seems to prefer the upstairs bedrooms and the stairway for her visits.

In 1992, Coy Dillon's boyhood friend and his wife—both school teachers—stayed at Grace Hall and awoke to find an old gentleman standing by the closet door. When they asked him what he was doing, he disappeared. That, and Selma's other odd stories, prompted a TV network to do a program about the town. A psychic on the TV team who stayed at the inn was also wakened by the old gentleman. In a separate incident, a disembodied voice inquired of the psychic, in a very southern drawl, "Why are you pokin' around here?"

While everyone else seemed to be meeting up with Miz Eliza and her fellow intangible residents, the Dillons still hadn't seen them. But in September 1994, all that changed. Says Coy Dillon:

"The weather was still quite warm and the sun was up early at about 6:00 A.M. As is my practice, at 5:00 A.M. I get up, go downstairs, shut off the porch lights, get coffee for myself and my wife, and return to my bedroom. However, when I returned to the bedroom, my old dog, Eloise, decided she wanted to go outside.

"Back down the stairs [he went] to the rear door. Just as I opened the door—by now it was approximately 5:30 A.M. and breaking daylight—I saw Miz Eliza walk across the porch and down the steps. I rapidly reached into the hallway to turn on the porch lights, but when I did, there was nothing more to see."

Since then, the Dillons have "identified" the old gentleman ghost as a Mr. Satterfield, an attorney who boarded at Grace Hall for many years and fell in love with one of Miz Eliza's daughters, Miss Mary. Because there was a vast age difference, the couple never married. But when he died, Mr. Satterfield left all his money to Miss Mary.

"He resided at Grace Hall from the late 1800s until 1923, so it was a wonderful romance that lasted twenty-five years," Coy says. "We still have Mr. Satterfield's parlor chair and, quite possibly, he returns to 'put his feet up.' "

With four spirits safely identified, however, one mystery remains. According to the TV psychic, there are *five* ghosts at Grace Hall. One has yet to put in an appearance. Coy Dillon, by now quite used to his intangible guests, is intrigued.

"I wonder," he says, "who the last spirit is."

GRACE HALL

Address:	506 Lauderdale Street, Selma, Alabama 36701
Telephone:	(205) 875-5744 or (334) 875-5744
Fax:	(334) 875-9967
Facilities:	Beautifully restored bed-and-breakfast
Price Range:	Inexpensive

KENDALL MANOR

Eufaula, Alabama

KENDALL MANOR, one of the many beautiful and historic homes built in the days when cotton was king, stands majestically on the hillside along West Broad Street, just two-and-a-half blocks from the city center. Built by James Turner Kendall in the mid-1800s, it is perhaps the most impressive residence in town: constructed in Italianate style with sixteen-foot ceilings, gold leaf cornices, an Italian marble fireplace, and ruby-colored glass windows.

The house has become a landmark because of the distinctive belvedere, or white tower, which crowns the two-story structure.

Guest rooms contain either antique or queen-size four-poster beds and are furnished with antiques. All have private baths.

Southern hospitality starts the moment a guest arrives. There's afternoon tea served in the parlor or a welcome drink in the library. Unusual for a bed-and-breakfast, Kendall Manor provides a turn-down service, and there is a full breakfast which includes fresh home-baked bread and muffins and a selection of seasonal fruits.

Altogether, Eufaula has more than seven hundred historic and architecturally significant buildings, including Alabama's domestic Italianate architecture and an impressive collection of mid- to late-nineteenth-century, small-town commercial buildings.

The annual Eufaula Pilgrimage and Antique show in April is a big attraction which celebrates this heritage. The Indian Summer Festival in October is an equally popular occasion. Nearby places to visit are the forty-six-thousand-acre Lake Eufaula, with its 640 miles of shoreline nestling in the Chattahoochee River Valley; the nearby Eufaula National Wildlife Refuge; and Tom Mann's Fish World attraction.

THE GHOST at Kendall Manor is Annie, a nursemaid to the children of the house in its early days, whose fearsome reputation was passed down from generation to generation. The house's owners, Timothy and Barbara Lubsen, say, "It was well known that Annie, a favorite, was very concerned with her charges and kept an eagle eye on the youngsters in her care. No one could get away with anything when Annie was around."

The great-great-great-grandsons of James Turner Kendall, for whom the house was built, had heard these stories. One day, while the young lads were racing noisily around the veranda on their tricycles, the youngest boy glanced up at the dining-room window and saw Annie standing there "with her hands on her hips, and in her black dress and starched apron."

The boy was so frightened that he lost control of his tricycle and fell off, suffering scrapes and bruises. But at least that strict spirit had stopped him racing. "To this day, he swears Annie was there, and won't go by the window," the Lubsens say.

When Kendall Manor was first built, the servants also told of another ghost: a man on a white horse who appeared only when something bad was going to happen. The Kendalls tended to scoff at the tales of this harbinger of doom, a tall man wearing a gray uniform and a broad-brimmed hat. But when James Turner Kendall's manservant, Logan, spotted the stranger and ran into the house to tell Mrs. Kendall of his sighting, they had reason to think again. "Something's going to happen," cried Logan. And it did. Kendall died the next day.

KENDALL MANOR

Address:	534 West Broad Street, Eufaula, Alabama 36027
Telephone:	(205) 687-8847
Facilities:	Bed-and-breakfast combining southern hospitality with a historic setting
Price range:	Inexpensive

WOODLAND PLANTATION
Moundville, Alabama

SITUATED ON two hundred acres of private forest, Woodland is an eighteen-room mansion built in the transitional style. It now operates as a very comfortable bed-and-breakfast. It is furnished throughout with family antiques, and boasts a number of original family portraits by Confederate artist Nicola Marschall—designer of both the Confederate army uniform and the Stars and Bars Confederacy flag.

All the guest bedrooms, which are on the second floor, have private bathrooms and overlook the flower-filled grounds, orchards, and woods. Early risers will spot deer on the grounds. Picking your own fruit in the orchard is permitted—as is fishing in the four-acre, spring-fed lake stocked with huge bass and bream. There is also skeet shooting on the grounds and an on-site antique shop.

Fancy a stroll? Then one of the resident golden retrievers—E. J., Georgia, Yuppie, or Moseby—will be delighted to accompany you. This is wonderful country for exploring, full of history. When the lake was being dug, artifacts dating back fifteen thousand years were discovered.

The mansion contains a library of hundreds of volumes, which is a nice convenience for bad-weather days. There are no TV sets in the bedrooms, but innkeeper E. P. (Buck) Whatley says guests are welcome to join him in front of his set, in the spacious kitchen, to watch the news or selected programs. He is also available for "lively conversation." Full breakfasts are provided, and an afternoon cocktail is offered by the innkeeper.

Local attractions include the University of Alabama; the county seat of Greensboro; a number of beautiful houses that are open to the public; and the 360-acre Native American prehistoric site and museum at Mound State Monument in Moundville.

THE GHOST at Woodland is an anonymous spirit who perhaps once lived in the old plantation house and who still turns the lights on and off and moves furniture around.

"I have never dwelled on the fact that I live in a ghost-inhabited house—though I must admit I have a great deal of fun watching guests' expressions as I recount the tales," says the present owner, Buck Whatley. Buck grew up on the plantation and takes a philosophical view of his nonpaying guests.

"Most people equate ghosts with evil apparitions set on hurting or frightening us space-and-time-bound humans," he says. "Woodland's ghosts are not like that."

Nor have they ever been. When Buck's mother told an elderly black plantation worker that her children had seen ghosts, he replied, "Well, Missus, ain't no reason for Cap'n Buck to be scared. Any ghosts dare gon' be kin to 'im an' dey ain't gon' hut 'im."

Today, Whatley freely admits that many of the old plantation workers delighted in tales of ghosts and "haunts" and particularly enjoyed teasing the children with them. Such a childhood is bound to leave a lasting impression. But when Whatley's father died, the family moved away. The plantation was rented out to people who had never heard the old stories. They, too, experienced strange, inexplicable goings-on, such as lights turning themselves on and off despite being disconnected. One tenant family fled Woodland in the middle of the night, refusing to remain in "a haunted house."

Buck, his wife, and their infant son returned to Woodland in 1972, "to restore it and make it once again home to the Whatleys." They found the building gutted. "All plumbing fixtures had been stolen,"

Buck recalls. "All copper pipes had been taken—I'm sure to be used as a still to brew spirits of another kind." Entire walls had been ripped out by people seeking the fabled, nonexistent family treasure.

Camping out in the ruins on their first night home, the Whatleys found that whenever they turned off the light in their room, it came back on.

"I took a flashlight and crawled under the house to check for electrical problems," Buck recalls. "Finding none, I returned to bed and turned the light off again. When it came back on, all we could do was laugh. The ghosts were welcoming us back home.

"This ghostly greeting was but the first of a number of unexplainable happenings we experienced at Woodland over the next twenty-five years. Shortly after we finished restoring the house and moved our furniture in, we began to realize that our scheme of decorating was not to everyone's liking. Or at least not to the liking of at least one friendly spirit."

A nineteenth-century engraving of a pair of seagulls, which the Whatleys hung over the mission library table in the gallery, was twice taken down in the night by unseen hands and placed carefully on the table. Eventually, they took the hint and replaced the engraving with a seascape in oils. "This decision evidently met with ghostly approval," Buck says.

An old family sideboard in the eating area was used to store Buck's grandmother's Limoges china, just as it is now. Because his son Edward was still small, Buck used to lock the sideboard doors at night and hide the key in a drawer. But the doors were often found unlocked and open the next morning.

"Ghosts?" says Buck, "Yes, we do have ghosts. Strange little happenings are commonplace here. And sure, we tell tales about them and, from time to time, we embellish these tales. One has only to stay here for a while to experience things that are simply unexplainable."

WOODLAND PLANTATION

Address:	Route 2, Moundville, Alabama 35474
Telephone:	(205) 371-2734 or (205) 371-6590
Facilities:	Restored plantation house, fishing, antique shop
Price Range:	Inexpensive

COPPER QUEEN HOTEL

Bisbee, Arizona

A BEAUTIFUL OLD PROPERTY, "the Queen" was built by the Copper Queen Mining Company in the very early part of the twentieth century when Bisbee, high in the hills and close to the Mexican border, was the world's largest mining town. The Queen still dominates the attractive little town and is being lovingly restored to its original grandeur.

There are forty-five comfortable guest rooms, all with every modern convenience. The public rooms are particularly atmospheric: they include two lobbies, the traditionally styled Copper Queen Saloon, an excellent dining room, and a patio where meals and drinks are available. The hotel has its own swimming pool.

The townspeople still visit the Copper Queen for a cocktail or a few beers in the evening, just as they've always done. And although men such as "Black Jack" Pershing and the young Teddy Roosevelt, who once frequented the hotel, are long gone, the town's new settlers—artists, writers, and film-makers—are just as interesting to meet and talk with.

Bisbee's copper mines can still be visited. Outfitted with yellow slickers and miner's lamps, groups descend deep into the shafts of the abandoned Copper Queen Mine before catching the cramped mining train back to the surface. Tours are also available to the Lavender Pit Mine, one of the world's largest open pit mines.

Above ground, the clear skies and accommodating climate of this mile-high town make for great tennis, swimming, hiking, golf, and sight-seeing. Rock collectors go in search of mineral specimens, which include the famous "Bisbee Blue Turquoise." Souvenir shopping is excellent. Historic Tombstone, site of the famous shoot-out at the O.K. Corral, is just a twenty-minute drive away.

THE GHOST at the Copper Queen is that of an unknown but romantically inclined woman of indeterminate age, who seems to spend most of her time on the third floor. But strange happenings are a regular occurrence throughout the beautiful old building. So much so, in fact, that staff keep a huge ledger on the reception desk where both employees and guests are asked to record any odd happenings. It makes strange reading.

"Weird things have happened to people who work here," general manager Peter Pieth says. One recent employee was a night porter who watched in amazement as the main doors in the entrance hall swung open and a light appeared to emerge from one of the big mirrors in the lobby, move around, then float up the grand staircase and finally disappear.

Night auditor Carol Estrader—she also makes the hotel's famous fudge—is another who has experienced strange nocturnal phenomena. But she has a theory. "Whatever or whoever it is, it likes young guys," she says. That would seem to be borne out by the experience of a good-looking chief engineer at the hotel, who stepped into the empty elevator and was alarmed to find an invisible presence breathing heavily beside him. Or the hunky bodyguard, looking after a movie star staying at the Copper Queen, who left his room in terror and refused to return after repeatedly hearing a husky voice murmuring "Hello" in his ear.

The most haunted rooms are thought to be Room 305 and Room 315, although two women guests who stayed in Room 312 in October 1992 reported that a hat belonging to neither of them kept flying around the room—an occurrence reported elsewhere in the hotel. Other slightly less inexplicable oddities include radio alarm clocks with minds of their own, and odd buzzing noises. Two psychics stayed on the third floor intending to investigate, but they left saying the vibes were too intense.

Another who didn't remain at the hotel was a relief night porter named Roger, who made the following entry in the reception desk diary on June 10, 1992: "I am not crazy and I don't do drugs. I'm just a city boy who has lived here for one month, and I don't know anything about ghosts.

"But last night I was working in the office and I kept hearing the dining-room doors swinging. I checked it out, and there was nothing. Then, as I was walking back to my desk, I glanced into one of the mirrors in the lobby. I saw an old lady standing on the stairs watching me—I swear it. She had a black dress, like [one from] the 1920s, and a white shawl on her shoulders. When I turned around to look at her, she was gone."

General manager Peter Pieth says: "We don't know who the lady is. But we do know she likes men. Perhaps someone was once murdered on the third floor. In a mining town like this, lots of things have happened since 1902."

In the last couple of years, the ghost has been relatively quiet. Reported incidents have been limited to the comparatively unremarkable, such as trash cans moving around of their own accord. Perhaps the old lady, whoever she is, is conserving her energy as she awaits this beautiful hotel's centenary. Or, rather more ominously, perhaps she is waiting for the centenary of whatever happened to her in those dim and distant days when Bisbee was a roistering mining town rather than a secluded, atmospheric, upscale holiday resort.

COPPER QUEEN HOTEL

Address:	P.O. Box CQ, 11 Howell Avenue, Bisbee, Arizona 85603
Telephone:	(602) 432-2216
Fax:	(602) 432-4298
Facilities:	Colorful saloon and dining, swimming pool
Price Range:	Inexpensive to moderate

HOTEL VENDOME

Prescott, Arizona

A CHARMING and pleasantly restored 1917 lodging house, the Hotel Vendome has twenty-five newly designed bedrooms within its original walls. Each room has either a queen-size bed or twin beds, with its own bathroom and cable TV. There are also two-room suites available (price range: moderate).

The rooms have all been individually decorated to make the most of the available space and light. Original wide woodworking has been retained and is complemented by oak furnishings, period wallpapers, country-print fabrics, and brass ceiling fans. Bathrooms often contain old-fashioned tubs, but there are also spacious new "garden tubs," each, according to the hotel's owner, Rama Patel, "with its own shelf to hold a chilled carafe of fine wine."

The comfortable lobby has a cozy little bar in one corner, hand-fashioned in cherry by local craftsmen. It features a custom-made wine boutique, serving both domestic and imported wines and beers. In all, this is a simple property, but with a comfortable and relaxed atmosphere.

The mile-high town of Prescott is a comfortable drive from Flagstaff, Phoenix, or Tucson, and close to the beauty of Sedona and the mystery of Jerome. The town is noted for its ideal climate, its twenty thousand easy-living and friendly residents, and its enthusiasm for the great outdoors. And what an outdoors! Prescott is surrounded by the beautiful Bradshaw Mountains and the Ponderosa pines of Groom Creek.

Summers are mild, autumns crisp, and the sunsets spectacular in these parts. Local attractions include the holiday lighting of Prescott's Courthouse Plaza at Christmas, the excitement of Frontier Days on July 4, and the treasures in the historic Sharlot Hall Museum.

THE GHOST at the Hotel Vendome is Abby, who died in 1925 but still lives in Room 16. And Abby is not alone. She is accompanied by her cat, Noble.

Rama Patel, who recently bought the hotel, even refers to Room 16 as "Abby's Room." She explains that Abby was once the owner of the hotel but lost it when she didn't pay her taxes. The new owner, however, let her stay at the property, which she thought of as home. When Abby fell sick, she sent her husband out for some medicine but for reasons unknown he didn't return. Left alone, sick, and starving, Abby passed away in the room. So, it appears, did Noble.

Since then, guests staying in Room 16 have reported a variety of unexplained incidents. The TV set has gone on and off by itself, and amateur ghost-hunters reported "contacting" Abby in the room. As the stories spread, Mary Woodhouse, a reporter for the local newspaper, the *Daily Courier*, and photographer Marcy Rogers spent a night in the haunted room.

"I believe Abby paid me a visit," Woodhouse said afterward. The radiators kept turning off during the night, leaving the room feeling cold, and she was awakened by the sound of a cat meowing even though she couldn't find a trace of the animal.

Despite such incidents, Abby and Noble are likely to remain in Prescott for a long time to come.

"Abby is part of the Hotel Vendome," says Rama Patel. "We don't want her to leave."

HOTEL VENDOME

Address:	230 South Cortez Street, Prescott, Arizona 86301
Telephone:	(602) 776-0900
Facilities:	Restored lodging house with modern hotel rooms and bar
Price Range:	Inexpensive

OLD VAN BUREN INN

Old Van Buren, Arkansas

FORMERLY THE Crawford County Bank building, the Old Van Buren Inn was purchased in 1988 by Jackie Henningsen, who, while on vacation from California, saw the building and fell in love with it. She and her family and friends spent hours renovating the building and turning the ground floor into an excellent California-style restaurant.

The second floor was then transformed into a bed-and-breakfast. There are just three bedrooms; each is filled with hand-picked Victorian antique furniture. The beds are soft and comfortable. Rocking chairs and a selection of books in each room complete the relaxing atmosphere. The sunny bathroom, which has a double tub, is shared by the three rooms.

Henningsen lives on the property, which was described as "the ultimate building" when it was erected in 1889. A new high-pressure brick was used in its construction, and the fixtures and fittings included Tennessee Valley marble, hardwoods from around the world, and ornate tin work.

The restaurant is Henningsen's pride and joy. Open and sunny, it serves food as Californian as the South can get. Meals are light and flavorful: crisp light salads, bean sprouts and avocados, quiche, seafood sandwiches, and hot Texas chili. Desserts are homemade. Don't miss the apple dumpling. The restaurant is open all week, from 9:00 A.M. to 5:00 P.M. and from noon to 4:00 P.M. on Sundays.

Old Van Buren itself is great fun to explore—full of antique shops, handcrafts, and art galleries. There are several historic homes in the area worth visiting, and boating and fishing are popular pastimes on the Arkansas River.

THE GHOST of the Old Van Buren Inn is an unidentified but roaming spirit that inhabits the second story of the former bank building. Henningsen describes the spirit as an "unseen presence." But, she says, "He's friendly," and suggests that her guests should introduce themselves to him.

It would be surprising if such a building did not have a ghost. The former bank survived several attempted hold-ups and other robberies and was closed down in the Great Depression. It ended up as the local gas company's offices. During Prohibition it had another role. The third floor was a speakeasy. At least that's how the local stories go. Why else would there still be a peephole cut in the door?

The old building went on to become a dance hall and then a club before Henningsen began her loving restoration. Now, it is somewhere you can "bank" on having a nice visit.

OLD VAN BUREN INN

Address:	633 Main Street, Corner of 7th and Main, Old Van Buren, Arkansas
Telephone:	(501) 474-4202
Facilities:	Antique-filled rooms above excellent restaurant
Price Range:	Inexpensive

THE CARTER HOUSE

Eureka, California

THE CARTER HOUSE is a beautifully furnished bed-and-breakfast in a stylish reproduction Victorian mansion in this northern California seaport.

Innkeepers Mark and Christie Carter have furnished it in elegant style with period pieces culled from stock when, in the late 1980s, they lived in the then newly built house and ran an antiques business from home.

Today, bed-and-breakfast guests check in at the Hotel Carter and are then taken across the road to their rooms in The Carter House. The five rooms there are very spacious, bold in decor, and contain some wonderful early Victorian oak and walnut bedsteads and armoires. All the rooms have private baths.

There is a kitchen for guests to prepare light meals, and each room has an imaginatively selected "honesty basket" of snacks and drinks. Downstairs is a finely fitted dining room, which opens to the garden. The entrance floor has a comfortable lounge-library with panoramic views over the harbor. Modern works of art hang throughout, and it is a tribute to the Carter family's taste that the overall effect is that of an intimate art gallery.

The Hotel Carter's hospitality includes guests at The Carter House, of course. There is a complimentary glass of wine in the lobby each afternoon at 5:00 P.M. from Carter's six-hundred-strong wine list, served with cheeses and canapés. Evening snacks are offered, too, and there is an excellent buffet breakfast. The restaurant is open for dinner only from Thursday through Sunday, featuring soft fruits, vegetables, and herbs from the Carter garden. The highlight of the day is a visit with the chef at about 4:00 P.M. to discuss the day's harvest.

THE GHOST at The Carter House is not exactly an apparition; it's a set of extraordinary and somewhat chilling coincidences.

Innkeeper Mark Carter, already busy with the Hotel Carter, yearned to fill a vacant lot kitty-corner from it with a Victorian mansion where he could live with his family. He could visualize exactly the kind of house that would suit the corner plot. But where could he find an architect or a set of plans to recreate the distinctive Victorian-Gothic style he envisioned? Diligent inquiries over a prolonged period in the 1980s produced nothing that seemed quite right.

Eventually, a friend in San Francisco came across a folio of old architects' drawings: pages and pages of plans for mansions of all shapes and sizes, dating from the 1870s. Still, when Carter browsed through it, nothing seemed to fit his ideal.

Then, toward the end of the volume, there appeared a plan of a house drawn up by the Newsom brothers and built in 1884 for the Murphy family on Bush and Jones in San Francisco. Although the house is now demolished, it was exactly how Carter had imagined his dream house for the lot in Eureka, right down to the last scalloped shingle and fretwork dado.

Thus was born The Carter House in Eureka, a meticulous reincarnation of the Murphy House completed in 1989.

So what's spooky about that? Despite Mark Carter's long quest for exactly the right design for his vacant plot, the Newsom plans could easily have escaped his notice.

But Eureka just happens to have two other beautiful Newsom houses, both within a block of where The Carter House now stands. There is the hugely magnificent, masculine, and slightly reptilian Carson Mansion (now the exclusive Ingomar Club) and, opposite it, the stunning Carson House—more delicate, pastel toned, and known as "the Pink Lady."

Just coincidence? Suffice to say, The Carter House is the house that "asked" to be built.

THE CARTER HOUSE

Address:	1033 Third Street, Eureka, California, 95501
Telephone:	(707) 455-1390
Facilities:	Beautiful bed-and-breakfast, meals in Hotel Carter
Price Range:	Moderate

THE CLIFT HOTEL

San Francisco, California

OPENED IN 1915, the seventeen-story Clift remains one of the top hotels in San Francisco. It stands in the heart of the city, very close to
Union Square, and sets the standard for luxury accommodations and
attentive personalized service.

The 329 beautifully appointed guest rooms and suites are spacious, with high ceilings, restored moldings and woodwork, fine
Georgian reproductions, and marble bathrooms. Each room is climate
controlled and has a concealed TV set, two telephone lines, and windows opening to the crisp San Francisco air. There is personal butler
service, a rapid laundry service, children's programs, a baby-sitting
service, valet parking, a fitness room, part-time free limo service,
even pet care.

Famous for years, the French Room restaurant is still one of the
city's top dining spots. The magnificent art deco Redwood Room
cocktail lounge and piano bar is a San Francisco landmark and favorite
meeting place in its own right. It was built from a single, two-
thousand-year-old redwood tree from the forests of northern California and has been restored to its original luster.

There are also business facilities, as one would expect from a hotel
of this class. Rather more of a surprise is the beautiful chandelier-lit
lobby and reception area that doubles as a lounge where afternoon tea
is served. The lobby is full of treasures such as grandfather clocks and
ormolu chairs. One particularly charming touch is the red urn full of

flowers, standing in front of the huge Kalander painting of a romantic scene which features, yes, an urn full of flowers.

The Clift Hotel is superbly situated within a very short walk of the city center, the famed Geary Street theaters, and plenty of fine boutiques and upscale department stores. Chinatown and the financial district are easily accessible.

THE GHOST at The Clift Hotel is Robert Odell, a larger-than-life character who once owned the property. He haunts the rooftop Spanish Suite, a self-contained seven-hundred-square-foot apartment he used as a permanent residence.

The Clift takes its name from Frederick Clift, a lawyer whose father owned land at the corner of Geary and Taylor Streets at the time of the San Francisco earthquake on April 18, 1906. Soon after the quake, and the fire that followed, Frederick Clift inherited his father's land. At a time when the city was rebuilding itself, he resolved to erect a regally styled and earthquake-proof hotel on the city's center site.

Clift gave the job of designing his dream property to George Applegarth, an ambitious young architect. Applegarth—pioneering the use of steel-reinforced concrete—planned a property destined to profoundly affect much of San Francisco's architecture and the way the city looks today. The original twelve-story hotel opened in 1915, with Clift taking up residence in the rooftop stone bungalow, today the Spanish Suite (Room 1509).

Clift died in 1936, but before his death, various financial deals passed the property to a thirty-six-year-old Iowan venture capitalist, Robert Odell. Odell promptly ordered the closure and complete renovation of The Clift. When the hotel reopened in 1936, the magnificent Redwood Room was unveiled, as one of the prime examples of art deco in the entire Bay Area.

Odell moved into the Spanish Suite with his wife, Helen. He was an imposing man, six-foot-six in stature and with piercing eyes. Odell was extremely strong and many of his employees were terrified of him, especially when he had been drinking. Staff would sound an alarm to warn one another when he returned from a night on the town. His hobby was breaking horses, but more than that, he was a *bon vivant*. He and Helen and their new-look hotel were a sensation. The hotel restaurant, over which Odell kept close control, became one of the most fashionable in the city. The guest list read like an international *Who's Who.*

Success continued for years. Odell and his managers pioneered many of what are now accepted practices among top hoteliers. The Odell era did not end until June 1973, and Odell ended it by his own hand. He committed suicide in the Spanish Suite.

The stories began at once. Employees claimed the suite was haunted and refused to enter it. Some still won't venture there.

Guests, however, appear to be made of sterner stuff. One regular visitor often uses the Spanish Suite and admits she has seen the glass sliding door leading out onto the balcony slowly opening and closing by itself. She also says that items regularly disappear from her display table, even when the suite is empty and locked.

Another guest awoke in the Spanish Suite to see trash cans flying through the air. The alarmed guest called reception, and staff rushed up to the suite. The huge, double wooden doors began to open and close themselves. Staff and guest alike watched in astonishment as the doors finally slammed themselves shut with such force that the wood cracked. There were a couple of other dramatic sightings while this book was being written.

Odell "comes and goes" in the Spanish Suite, according to banqueting manager Marina Lee. A public relations spokeswoman adds, a trifle anxiously, "The ghost has never directed violence at a person." But she admits, "It's been up to a number of hijinks and has scared many people over the decades."

THE CLIFT HOTEL

Address:	495 Geary Street, San Francisco, California 94102
Telephone:	(415) 775-4700
Fax:	(415) 441-4621
Facilities:	Full range of luxury hotel facilities, including personal butler service and free limos
Price Range:	Expensive

HOTEL DEL CORONADO

Coronado, California

CORONADO ISLAND, situated in San Diego Bay and accessible by a two-mile long bridge, is famous for two things: its huge U.S. Navy base and the vast red-roofed Hotel del Coronado. Looking like "an oversized pigeon loft," in the words of one writer, "the Del" is said to have been the inspiration for the Emerald City in *The Wizard of Oz* and the setting for the classic Marilyn Monroe film *Some Like It Hot*—although in the latter case the scriptwriters moved it to Florida.

The hotel also has an odd place in history. It is believed to be where Edward, prince of Wales, first met Mrs. Wallis Simpson, then a U.S. Navy officer's wife, in the ballroom in 1920. Sixteen years later the Prince of Wales was to rock the British throne by abdicating to marry the by-then-divorced Mrs. Simpson.

Opened in 1888, the Del has grown into the largest resort property on the Pacific Coast. The hotel claims to have hosted more celebrities than any other hotel in the United States. It is a national historic landmark and is listed in the *National Register of Historic Places.*

As has always been the case, today's guests want for nothing. Every room in the main Victorian building has been painstakingly restored and is one of a kind in its decor. Modern rooms, like those in the Ocean Tower, blend the accouterments of the past with all modern amenities, including air conditioning. Rooms offer magnificent views of the Pacific Ocean, the cityscape of San Diego Bay, the yachts of Glorietta Harbor, and flower-filled courtyards containing such rarities as one of America's only dragon trees (a native of the Canary Islands).

The facilities seem endless. There are eight restaurants and lounges, including two top dinner venues: the Ocean Terrace with its panoramic Pacific views, and the opulent Crown Room with its gilt-edged china and tuxedo-clad waiters. There are heated pools, a spa, a series of waterfront tennis courts, and Coronado's nearby eighteen-hole bayside golf course. Seaborne activities available at the Del's boathouse include sailing, fishing, and whale-watching excursions.

THE GHOST at the Hotel del Coronado is Kate Morgan, who either committed suicide at the hotel or was murdered there by her husband on November 29, 1892. Kate's room, now Room 3312, is said to be haunted, as is a former maid's room, Room 3502. Kate also fiddles with the phones and tampers with the television—and before you laugh that off, it has to be said this is one of the best-documented and most famous of America's hotel ghost stories.

Kate, a beautiful brunette wearing black nineteenth-century clothes, has often been seen gliding down the hotel's corridors or standing by the windows as if waiting for someone. Perhaps that someone is her husband, the card shark Tom Morgan. When they were traveling through Los Angeles by train in November 1892, Kate told her husband she was pregnant. The couple quarreled and Tom disembarked, but he did promise to meet Kate in San Diego for Thanksgiving.

Kate, twenty-seven, checked into the Hotel del Coronado on Thanksgiving Day, November 24. For some reason, she gave her name as Lottie A. Bernard of Detroit. Her husband did not arrive to join her, and after a couple of days Kate complained of pains and might have induced an abortion. She then took a ferry to San Diego, bought herself a .44-caliber gun, and left a message for Tom at another hotel, the Hotel Brewster, before returning to the Coronado. No one knows what happened that night, but the next day Kate was found dead on the steps leading from the hotel's north entrance to a sandwalk. She had been shot in the head and a single bullet was missing from the gun in her hand. Suicide? Perhaps. But the bullet that killed Kate Morgan was a .38-caliber or .40-caliber, from a different gun.

More than one hundred years later, the mystery still has not been solved. In his book *The Legend of Kate Morgan: The Search for the Ghost of the Hotel del Coronado*, published in 1990, attorney Alan M. May concluded that Kate was murdered by her returning husband. A former army buddy of May's, Gerry Rush, has gone even further. He contends Tom Morgan also killed the maid (Room 3502) who looked after Kate—she disappeared the day after Kate's funeral.

One weakness of these theories is that Tom Morgan was never seen at the Hotel del Coronado. Nonetheless, the reports of strange happenings in Rooms 3312 and 3502 continue unabated. Local historian Richard Carico slept in one of the haunted rooms in 1988 and heard "faint murmurings." In 1990, Rush claimed, he heard a woman

HOTEL DEL CORONADO

crying in the corridor. When he asked her what was the matter, the woman replied, "I was murdered. It is not only Kate Morgan in the ground. It is I, the housekeeper." Parapsychologist Christopher Chacon can find nothing out of the ordinary in Kate's room, Room 3312, but says of Room 3502: "It's a classic haunting." Hotel public relations director Nancy Weisinger was in Room 3502 when *Ghostbusters* star Dan Aykroyd's brother Tom, who really is a ghostbuster, set up some scientific equipment in the room.

"I heard the ashtray flip over," she says, "and a glass shattered in the bathroom. It didn't just break; it was as if someone threw it."

Less dramatically, countless guests have reported strange faults on the telephones and inexplicable images appearing on their TV sets. May thought he saw Kate Morgan's face on his TV screen, but as he also decided that she was his great-great-grandmother, perhaps his evidence can be discounted.

In some ways, the stories of Kate Morgan and the ghost of the Del have suffered from being told too often. But one impressive witness was travel agent Jeanie Hawkins, a very down-to-earth businesswoman. When I told her that I was writing this book, she said, "I know a hotel in California that you must include. It is called the Hotel del Coronado. Now that really is haunted."

She arrived there late one evening on a business trip and went straight to bed in the old part of the hotel without hearing any of the Kate Morgan stories. She remembers: "I couldn't sleep. There was a presence in my room. I didn't know it was haunted when I arrived, but there is certainly something there. I have stayed in hotels all over the world, and I've never come across anything like it before."

Was it sad Kate who disturbed Hawkins's slumbers? Or her disappearing maid? Or simply jet lag? Perhaps we will never know.

HOTEL DEL CORONADO

Address:	1500 Orange Avenue, Coronado, California 92118
Telephone:	(619) 522-8000, or for information or reservations call (800) HOTEL-DEL
Fax:	(619) 522-8262
Facilities:	Full resort facilities in an historic setting
Price Range:	Expensive

AN ELEGANT VICTORIAN MANSION

Eureka, California

JUST WHEN YOU think California's booming bed-and-breakfast industry can't spring any more surprises, you discover this place: an elegant Victorian mansion which—just to make sure there is no confusion—calls itself An Elegant Victorian Mansion.

Just a few blocks from Eureka's historic "Old Town," and set in a quiet, genteel residential neighborhood, An Elegant Victorian Mansion is a restored architectural masterpiece. Designated a national historical landmark, the mansion offers guests a comfortable bed, a sumptuous breakfast, and the attentive hospitality of owners Doug and Lily Vieyra.

This is a lovely place. Arriving guests are met by "Jeeves," the butler (who, when I was there, bore a remarkable resemblance to Doug Vieyra), and are accommodated in one of four very comfortable bedrooms. Only one of the bedrooms has a private bathroom.

The public rooms—parlors, library, and sitting room—are open to guests. New replica carpets, wallpaper duplicated by the original manufacturers, and plenty of antiques make, in the words of the Vieyras, "a living history museum." The atmosphere is nice, too—there is usually classical music playing in the background, and Doug Vieyra is an amusing conversationalist.

Breakfast is a gourmet meal, reflecting the style of a house whose history goes back to 1888. Although it is not suitable for children or smokers, the highlight of An Elegant Victorian Mansion is its family atmosphere, plus the company of hosts who describe themselves—with considerable accuracy—as "gregarious and congenial." Eureka, a former logging town with a new lease on life, has many splendid houses. An Elegant Victorian Mansion is one living up to its name.

THE GHOST at An Elegant Victorian Mansion (known locally and rather more prosaically as "The Clark Cottage") is that of an unknown and unseen woman with a taste for traditional jazz.

You couldn't find a more down-to-earth couple than the house's owners. Indeed, Doug Vieyra is a retired schoolteacher who had not even considered his home might be haunted. But then one evening a few years ago, a woman guest told the Vieyras she was a medium and the rear parlor had a spirit in it. She offered to release the "trapped" spirit, but the Vieyras, believing she was talking nonsense, politely declined.

"Since that time, a number of guests have reported strange happenings," Doug says. There was the woman guest in the Van Gogh Room, for example, who knocked on the Vieyras' bedroom door one night early in 1995 to complain that "a ghost had opened her door." Vieyra advised her to lock it, but the door again opened. He then advised her to bolt it, but the door again opened. The woman was considerably shaken—it's worth adding that by profession she was a reputable forensic scientist. Furthermore, I inspected the door less than two months after the incident, and it is impossible to see how it can be opened by anyone or anything once bolted.

But an even more mysterious incident happened the previous year when the Vieyras were away at an innkeepers' convention and left a woman friend house-sitting.

"When we got back, she told us she had been awakened by music coming from downstairs," Doug says. "It went on for some time, then stopped and started again."

An Elegant Victorian Mansion is equipped with an electronic alarm system. The house-sitter knew it was impossible for anyone to have broken into the property without her knowing. So, assuming that she had left a radio or TV set on, she got out of bed and went downstairs with a flashlight to see what was happening.

She found an old, hand-cranked horn phonograph playing by itself.

"That just can't happen," Vieyra says. "But it did."

He pointed out the phonograph and explained how it had to be wound between each playing. The house-sitter had heard it play twice, so it must have been wound twice. Moreover, whoever—or whatever—played the machine had carefully chosen the pride of Vieyra's record collection: a 1928 recording of the Duke Ellington band playing "St. Louis Blues" with, says Vieyra, "Crosby crooning, Armstrong on trumpet, and Benny Goodman on the clarinet." The alarmed house-sitter spent the rest of the night cowering on the stairs.

Oddly, after all this, the Vieyras remain skeptics. As her husband told the phonograph story, Lily Vieyra commented, "I would love that to happen to me. Then I could become a believer."

Strange happenings continue. Doors in the house seem to open of their own accord, then slam shut again. Things disappear. "Big things, like fruit bowls," Lily Vieyra says. "We say that the house is playing with us again." Her husband adds, "I expect there is a logical explanation, but I haven't worked it out yet."

Does that mean the Vieyras are regretting their decision not to let the medium free the "trapped" spirit in the rear parlor? Apparently not.

"If we have a ghost," says Doug Vieyra, "it's a nice ghost. I have someone I can work with here!"

AN ELEGANT VICTORIAN MANSION

Address:	1406 "C" Street, 14th and "C" Streets, Eureka, California 95501
Telephone:	(707) 444-3144
Facilities:	Historic bed-and-breakfast with friendly atmosphere
Price Range:	Inexpensive to moderate

GINGERBREAD MANSION INN

Ferndale, California

THIS IS AN extraordinary bed-and-breakfast in an extraordinary village. Both seem to have been left behind in a time warp. Visitors take a step back into the elegant Victorian age one hundred years ago.

The Gingerbread Mansion itself is one of the most photographed buildings in northern California. Built in 1898 as a doctor's residence, it later became a hospital. Exquisitely decorated with "gingerbread" trim, the beautiful Queen Anne/Eastlake Victorian property has been lovingly restored by owner Ken Torbert (who also landscaped the grounds) to create one of the most exquisite bed-and-breakfasts in America.

The process is ongoing. But it would be hard to find a speck of dust anywhere in the house, or a leaf out of place in the manicured garden.

There are eleven guest bedrooms in this state historic landmark, including four spectacular suites. They are all beautifully furnished, all have private bathrooms with showers, and they come filled with extras like toweling robes and the wherewithal for bubble baths. Room rates include a delicious afternoon tea in one of the parlors, as well as a full breakfast featuring homemade dishes. No children under ten years of age, no pets, and no smoking indoors are the house rules.

Youngsters would be bored by Ferndale anyway. But for adults it is a constant delight: a Victorian treasure house of historic homes, churches, and other buildings. Even the shops seem stuck in another age, fun to explore. The town does put on lively theatrical performances. But voyages of exploration on foot, or on the bicycles that Torbert keeps for guests, are the principal pastime. History is all around you. At the Gingerbread Mansion you will be staying in the best-looking bit of it.

THE GHOSTS at the Gingerbread Mansion Inn are presumed to be a couple of mischievous Victorian children, although nobody is quite sure who exactly they were, when they lived there, or what they are doing. Suffice it to say they have picked wonderful surroundings, for the Gingerbread Mansion is one of the best-preserved and most beautifully kept Victorian houses in the United States.

"When I bought the house, it had been empty for years," innkeeper Ken Torbert says. A former corporate planning analyst, he used to visit inns on his own holidays, and when he was driving past the Gingerbread Mansion and saw a For Sale sign up outside, he simply fell in love with it. "When I first walked into the place, even though I am a Victorian buff, it had a sense of space and balance—and I knew I wanted to live here. I love it," Torbert says.

There was a problem, however. Local people, especially youngsters, avoided the derelict old house, a former nurses' home, because they believed it was haunted.

"Every town has a haunted house, and in Ferndale it was this one," says Larry Martin, who grew up in the town and now works as the inn's chef.

Undaunted, Torbert started a painstaking and extremely thorough restoration—and the house is now immaculate. The ghostly youngsters, if they are still around, should be pleased with their home—but odd things happen. A picture which Torbert hung in the front parlor mysteriously moved itself into the lounge.

Guests walking up the main staircase have slipped on the slightly short thirteenth stair and claimed they were pushed. And one guest, Christopher Earls, spending the night of his twentieth birthday in a suite, awoke "too frightened to turn over" because he "thought there was something there."

Torbert's wife, Sandie, tells of two women guests who arrived from San Francisco saying they had come to the Gingerbread Mansion because their friends had "talked about the children."

Children? Sandie has just one daughter. But Torbert can add to the story: "We had some touched-up photos of Victorian children with somber faces," he recalls. "Sometimes, guests would stay up late and write long entries in the guest books which we have in each room. They wrote about the children, who 'came alive at night.' "

It is hard to imagine a more peaceful and comfortable inn. Relax, and the mind plays tricks. And there can be few more relaxing places than the Gingerbread Mansion Inn.

GINGERBREAD MANSION INN

Address:	P.O. Box 40, 400 Berding Street
	Ferndale, California 95536
Telephone:	(707) 786-4000
Facilities:	Historic bed-and-breakfast in historic village
Price Range:	Moderate

HAUS KLEEBAUER

San Francisco, California

OPENING ITS OWN "golden gate" in San Francisco is the atmospheric Haus Kleebauer bed-and-breakfast, situated in Noe Valley about two miles from downtown. Small shops, coffee houses, and galleries line the main street of this village-style section of the city—and the Haus Kleebauer's greatest recommendation is its high percentage of return guests.

Constructed in 1892 by Austrian builder Frederick Kleebauer and his sons, Haus Kleebauer is a storybook-style Victorian home which retains all its original charm. Stained- and etched-glass windows, elaborate exterior trim, and manicured gardens recall an earlier era of elegance and charm.

This bed-and-breakfast has only two guest rooms, one of them a single, but visitors are looked after with meticulous thoroughness by the hospitable owners, Don Kern and Howard Johnson. A wine-and-cheese welcome, fresh flowers and fruit in the room, home-made chocolate chip cookies and other snacks, and an evening turndown service are unusual touches for a bed-and-breakfast. The delicious breakfasts are served in guests' rooms.

Children and pets are welcome at the Haus Kleebauer, and the attraction of this base to families is underlined by the fact that there is free on-street parking right outside, while the streetcar to the center of San Francisco takes only about fifteen minutes.

This means that the cosmopolitan round-the-clock attractions of San Francisco are all within easy reach. Old favorites include the Golden Gate Bridge, cable-car rides (plus a visit to the Cable Car Museum), and shopping. Returning visitors might not yet have seen the marvelous new Museum of Modern Art, right opposite the convention center. If that has only whetted your appetite, Haus Kleebauer can arrange bus tours with front-door pick-up or limo services.

THE GHOST at Haus Kleebauer is Miss Libby—an old english sheepdog who loved the house so much, she seems to have remained there after her death.

"She was a rescue dog," co-owner Don Kern explains. "We got her eight years ago, when she was already seven or eight years old. We saved her from being put to sleep, and during the time she lived with us and our other dog, Nura, a wire-haired fox terrier, Miss Libby became like a person."

Miss Libby died in 1994.

"But I believe she is still with us," Kern says. "We have often felt her brush past us."

Imagination? If so, Nura is imagining it, too. She watches the same invisible figure cross the room.

What's more, guests who knew Miss Libby support the idea that she is still there. Because of their long coats, old english sheepdogs often get hair over their eyes, cannot see very well, and walk into things. Both Don Kern, his partner, Howard Johnson, and regular visitors have heard the distinctive sound of Miss Libby bumping into the furniture upstairs. When these noises occur, Nura, an alert watchdog, does not stir. One other oddity: Kern and Johnson still frequently find an imprint in the shape of a large dog on the bed where Miss Libby customarily slept.

"It's kind of weird, sometimes," Kern says with admirable restraint. But at least the see-through sheepdog has resulted in one advantage for dog-owning guests. Well-behaved dogs are warmly welcomed.

"But," Kern says, "we cannot guarantee how other people's dogs will react to Miss Libby."

HAUS KLEEBAUER

Address: 225 Clipper Street, San Francisco, California 94114
Telephone: (415) 821-3866
Facilities: City center bed-and-breakfast with many extras
Price Range: Inexpensive

HORTON GRAND

San Diego, California

THE HORTON GRAND used to be the Grand Horton. It also used to be the Brooklyn. Both of these hotels, built in 1886, were part of a boom in San Diego's history. Modern-day developer Dan Pearson got the idea of giving both old properties a new lease on life by pulling them down and using the parts to create a new hotel. The result is the Horton Grand, an ultramodern property opened in 1986 with many original Victorian features.

The hotel, at the heart of the historic Gaslamp Quarter, is an impressive, four-story building consisting of two "wings" connected at street level by a modern glass atrium that encloses the lobby. The two wings differ. The one on the right as you face the hotel is straightforward Victorian; the one on the left is slightly more elegant with a touch of gingerbread styling. The external brickwork, bay windows, door frames, and internal main stairway all date from 1886.

There are 132 guest rooms, including twenty-four suites. All are equipped with fireplaces from the old properties and furnished with antiques. There are concealed TV sets.

Public rooms offer the same mixture of old-style elegance with a fresh, modern feel. The Ida Bailey Restaurant—named after a famous San Diego madam and hostess—features classic American cuisine, while the Palace Bar has become a mecca for fans and performers of international mainstream jazz. Two culinary standouts are the hotel's award-winning Sunday brunches and the hugely popular English high tea served every day except Sunday and Monday (reservations are advised).

For sightseeing trips around San Diego, horse-drawn carriages and the Old Town trolleys are right outside the main entrance. The Horton Plaza shopping center and the convention center are two blocks away.

THE GHOST at the Horton Grand is deceased gambler Roger Whittaker, murdered for his money more than a hundred years ago. He haunts Room 309—which is a mystery in itself because he had nothing to do with that room, or indeed the hotel, when he was alive. He just feels comfortable there, suggest psychics Shelley Deegan and Jacqueline Williams.

Almost immediately after the bits and pieces of the old San Diego hotels were used to construct the Horton Grand Hotel, staff started to complain that "strange things were going on" in Room 309. The lights went on and off of their own accord; a bed shook; pictures were moved around when the room was empty.

"What really got me one day was when a closet door flew open," former housemaid Martha Mayes says. "I never saw a ghost, but some people say they did."

Those people include a woman guest who walked down the hallway looking for the ice machine, stopped to ask a man if he knew where it was, then watched in open-mouthed amazement as the man faded into nothingness. There was also the case of a woman who stayed in Room 309 with her young daughter and found the child playing with an invisible companion.

"Don't you see him?" the puzzled little girl asked.

Ghost-hunters and reporters galore have stayed in Room 309 and have emerged with stories of being pushed and pulled by an invisible entity.

"I feel as if Roger is still here, here in this room," one exclaimed excitedly.

Unfortunately, Roger was never in that room. Nor was he in either of the hotels from which the Horton Grand was built. Both were constructed after his murder. Whittaker—who liked to describe himself as a "dude"—was murdered at age thirty-seven by a fellow gambler and robbed of his money.

Perhaps because it is a relatively new property, investigations into the phenomena at the Horton Grand have been unusually thorough.

Whittaker is believed to have been hiding in an armoire when he was murdered, and there is an armoire in Room 309. But it is not the same armoire. Perhaps he was murdered in a building that once stood on the site? Impossible—the site was under water 150 years ago.

"This room just reminds him of his room," psychic Jacqueline Williams explains.

Deegan goes somewhat further and claims that while she was walking up the spiral staircase to the third floor, she once met a group of fifteen or twenty ghosts. She told a popular newspaper, "They were all dressed in the style of the 1890s and were having a dance."

Such claims, one might reckon, do little for the credibility of the Horton Grand's ghost story. There is also the fact that Roger the lodger is undoubtedly good for business. Offers to exorcise him have been turned down, and Room 309 has bookings for years to come.

"This," says Deegan, a trifle unnecessarily perhaps, "is a good place for ghosts."

The ghosts seem to be good for bringing in the customers, too.

HORTON GRAND

Address:	Three-Eleven Island Avenue, San Diego, California 92101
Telephone:	(619) 544-1886, or for information and reservations (800) 542-1886
Fax:	(619) 239-3823
Facilities:	Very modern, but with original Victorian features
Price Range:	Expensive

THE MACCALLUM HOUSE

Mendocino, California

PERCHED ON rugged coastal cliffs with a backdrop of redwood and cypress forests, Mendocino is an extremely pretty little town full of picket-fenced Victorian houses and old redwood water towers. The water towers provide the clue: this was once a lumber mill town.

The MacCallum House, built in 1882 by William MacCallum for his newlywed daughter, Daisy, is a comfortable preservation of the old way of life. It was restored in 1974, but original tiffany lamps and intricate persian rugs—still in place—help transport guests back to another time. There is warm redwood paneling everywhere.

Twenty-two bedrooms were counted upon inspection of the property, and they did not all have private facilities. Work was in progress to reduce the number of rooms to twenty, all with private baths. Prices vary considerably according to the accommodation, but all the rooms are comfortable and atmospheric.

Predinner drinks on the porch of the Gray Whale Bar offer seasonal views of gray whales. They migrate twice annually, passing close to the shore, and are an impressive sight. The MacCallum House Restaurant, with its huge old cobblestone fireplace, has a varied menu of creative cuisine.

Although Mendocino is a quiet little town, visitors seem to find plenty to do—gallery browsing, beachcombing, fishing, hiking, tennis, skin diving, and, of course, whale-watching. But the favored pastime is just relaxing.

THE GHOST at The MacCallum House is Donald MacCallum, the somewhat repressed son of the MacCallum family. It seems Donald was prevented by his strict mother, Daisy, from enjoying either a fulfilled life or any kind of satisfying sexual relationship. His former bedroom is now Room 6—and lone women guests sleeping in that room have suffered (or perhaps enjoyed) the attentions of the frustrated Donald.

THE MACCALLUM HOUSE

The bad news for Donald is that his mother still has her eyes on him, for some say she still haunts the house that was built for her when she was a bride back in 1882.

Dirty Donald was caught by his mother while exercising his lust for life in the greenhouse—now the Greenhouse Suite. She never let him forget this embarrassing moment. Nor did she let him escape from her maternal apron strings, and although he worked briefly in a bank, he ended up a bachelor whose only employment was as his mother's chauffeur.

Lady friends were definitely off the menu. But who knows what naughty thoughts passed through Donald's mind as he lay alone in his room? And who knows why women guests in Room 6 sometimes report having erotic dreams and the feeling of sharing the room with an unknown man?

"To put it bluntly," says receptionist and local historian Christo Earls, "a certain amount of groping goes on in there."

The room's reputation has spread. Some women guests specifically request it. One woman watched in amazement as an unseen hand pushed her husband out the door and slammed it shut behind him.

"There are so many stories," says Earls. "A psychic has told us there is a presence in the house, and employees certainly believe there is."

Earls himself went into Room 6 to lock up late one night when it was empty. He says, "It was like walking into a refrigerator. It was horrible. My hair stood on end. It felt as if there was someone there. I got out quickly."

His surprise was matched by a couple of late-night partygoers who returned to the hotel not long ago to find an old woman sitting in reception. "Hello," said the old lady—then disappeared into what used to be Daisy's room. The guests followed her and found the room—Room 5—empty. Thoroughly frightened, they checked out immediately and drove to another hotel seven miles up the road.

Lots of Daisy's possessions are still in the hotel. So are Donald's rock and shell collections, which are kept in an attic. An attempt was made to display the collection in the lobby fairly recently, but then a disembodied voice informed the hotel owner's son that "Donald wants them back." They were put back in the attic.

Daisy MacCallum was a wealthy and matriarchal figure who became something of a local heroine in northern California during the aftermath of the San Francisco earthquake in 1906, going out to feed the homeless in person and setting up various charities. She was also a keen churchgoer. But she presided over a divided family and mothered a weak son. And the reverberations of those stresses and strains still echo around her comfortable old home.

THE MACCALLUM HOUSE

Address:	P.O. Box 206, 45020 Albion Street, Mendocino, California 95460
Telephone:	(707) 937-0289, or for the restaurant (707) 937-5763
Facilities:	Victorian bed-and-breakfast with many original furnishings, restaurant
Price Range:	Inexpensive to moderate

MADRONA MANOR

Healdsburg, California

THE SPECTACULAR Madrona Manor was built by the entrepreneur John Alexander Paxton in the 1880s and turned into a country inn and restaurant in 1982 by John and Carol Muir. While John Muir was working in Saudi Arabia, they spent their spare time designing an inn with Spanish/Moorish influence. The plan was to erect it once they returned home. But the Muirs could not find a suitable site and then fell in love with the faded elegance of the Madrona Knoll Rancho.

Helped by a crew of carpenters, they turned the old Victorian house into a beautiful and exceedingly elegant inn. In many ways, the work goes on—for work on a property like Madrona Manor is never complete.

The inn is a family affair. The Muirs, a charming couple, are the innkeepers; son Todd, whose cooking has been internationally acclaimed, is executive chef; son Mark is maintenance man; and eldest son Rob is a partner in the undertaking. Daughter Denice has worked there as pastry chef, and son-in-law John Fitzgerald was the landscape designer. The latter pair have now moved on, but it is evident that Fitzgerald did a superb job. The gardens are glorious.

There are nine spacious and comfortable bedrooms in the original three-story mansion, many of them furnished with antiques, plus a selection of five suites and cottages in outbuildings. All the bedrooms have full private facilities, air conditioning, hair dryers, and are individually decorated. The Music Room in the old house is a lounge for guests—it has a fireplace, piano, and ongoing giant jigsaw puzzle. Madrona Manor is listed in the *National Register of Historic Places.*

The inn is a perfect base for exploring the Sonoma wine country.

THE GHOST at Madrona Manor is an unknown woman dressed in black who might be the former owner, Hannah Paxton. Tradition says she is most likely to be seen in Room 201, "the haunted bedroom." But journalist Carolyn Yarborough, from San Diego, reported in the *Los Angeles Times* in 1985 that she had awakened to find a mysterious figure, illuminated by a shaft of light from under the bathroom door, standing by her bed in the house's only ground-floor bedroom, Room 101.

"She was very clear," Yarborough wrote. "She was wearing a long black dress with a white Peter Pan collar fastened with a narrow black ribbon. I had the impression she was youngish—perhaps mid-thirties."

Yarborough was considerably shocked. "I closed my eyes and forced myself to breathe more slowly," she wrote. "When I was more in control, I opened my eyes with fearful trepidation. The woman had moved. She was sitting in the blue velvet chair by the window."

Yarborough asked the woman what she wanted, and the figure slowly faded away.

This detailed description by a trained observer, coupled with Yarborough's honest admission of her own fear, has given this report unusual veracity. But it's not the only one of its kind. In 1986, the American Automobile Association magazine *Motorland* referred to the house containing "the resident ghost of a strange lady dressed in black." The Muirs have not seen her, but staff and guests have.

If Hannah Paxton is indeed the ghost, why did the strange woman (who once walked into the Rose Room dining room through the French windows and told guests she approved of what the Muirs had done) say her name was Elsie? And why do fire alarms go off in the stable without reason?

One slightly mysterious guest was alarmed by the atmosphere in the house and sent Carol Muir some crystals to bury under the porch and the front door. Carol Muir obliged and admits, "I haven't seen a ghost since, but then I hadn't seen one before." Chalk one up for this real-life *Ghost and Mrs. Muir.*

Psychics have said there are "all sorts of spirits" around the old house, although it seems to offer an exceptionally warm, comfortable, and friendly atmosphere. The Muirs themselves have experimented by sleeping in Room 101 and Room 201, but their nights were uneventful. They do say, however, there is "something of a mystery" about Room 201 in that it is possible to walk behind the wall by the fireplace—an architectural oddity for no apparent reason.

One other oddity concerns the fate of Hannah Paxton's husband. The local story is that when he died, he was put in a lead-lined coffin, laid in state in Room 203, then buried in the gardens.

The Muirs are not dismayed. Keen gardeners themselves, they found no trace of a grave—marked or unmarked. And when their neighbors saw the report in the *Los Angeles Times* and asked the Muirs whether they worried about the effect on business, Carol Muir threatened to "invent a few more." She says, decisively, "People like ghosts."

MADRONA MANOR

Address:	1001 Westside Road, P.O. Box 818, Healdsburg, California 95448
Telephone:	(707) 433-4231 or (800) 258-4003
Fax:	(707) 433-0703
Facilities:	Elegant country inn and restaurant in Sonoma wine country
Price Range:	Moderate

THE MANSIONS

San Francisco, California

THE MANSIONS HOTEL and Restaurant describes itself, with some accuracy, as "the world's wackiest hotel." Although it is only minutes away from the attractions of downtown San Francisco, it is also a million miles from the real world. For in this Victorian setting, consisting of two houses linked together to form a hotel, there is a world of mystery and magic.

The property is owned and run by Robert Pritikin who, besides being a hotelier, is an adman, author, and musician. He says, "I don't sell hotel rooms. I sell romance, surprises and outrage."

To that end, he has filled The Mansions with treasured antiques, fine art, and a superb collection of historic documents. He also stages predinner magic shows. The latter, included in the room price, can be followed by an excellent four-course dinner in a dining room decorated with rare sculptures and an extraordinary collection of Spanish stained-glass panels. Dinner reservations are essential.

THE MANSIONS

A full breakfast, a surprise gift for every guest, a magic museum—no wonder Pritikin counts many world-famous show-business stars among his guests.

There are twenty-one beautifully furnished guest rooms, including several suites. All are different, with period furniture, antiques, tapestries, and great paintings. All have a private bath, telephone, and other modern amenities. Breakfast is served in bed, or in the country kitchen.

The cable car is four blocks away, and the buses run from the hotel to Union Square, North Beach, and Fisherman's Wharf. Nearer to home, the streets around the hotel contain some of San Francisco's most splendid homes and local shops. In the hotel itself, Pritikin—who describes himself as America's foremost sawist—might pick out a tune for you on the handyman's saw. Favorite numbers include "The Last Time I Sawed Paris" and "Moonlight Sawnata."

THE GHOST at The Mansions is thought to be that of Claudia Chambers, the niece of Senator Chambers who, in 1887, built one of the houses that now comprise the hotel.

"Many guests have encountered her there," Pritikin says.

According to Pritikin, the psychics Lorraine and Ed Warren of Amityville fame told him the magic shows in the hotel were "exacerbating the situation" by celebrating ghosts. The appearance of "Claudia" as a disembodied, talking head during the magic show's dramatic finale is certainly a gruesome and otherworldly illusion.

Ghosthunters galore have been made welcome at The Mansions and reported mysterious "activity" on the third floor.

"That is also the area where guests volunteer, unsolicited, their experiences," Pritikin says. "I have never seen anything myself, but I have to be a believer. I hear so much evidence from guests."

Psychic Sylvia Brown, who went into a trance in the hotel in 1991, spoke of the house once having been a brothel and described a girl in a turn-of-the-century maid's uniform whose presence could be felt "like brushing against cobwebs." During another trance in the hotel's Empress Josephine Suite in 1992, the ouija board "went wild." Two wine glasses fifteen feet away shattered and dissolved into lumps of molten glass. The remains of the glasses are still on display in the Billiard Room.

Strange indeed. But the psychics agree, "the entities are not harmful." And whether or not Claudia, or any other young ladies, are really roaming the house in spirit form, Claudia will certainly put in an appearance for anyone attending Pritikin's preprandial performance in the library.

THE MANSIONS

Address:	2220 Sacramento Street, San Francisco, California 94115
Telephone:	(415) 929-9444
Facilities:	Magic shows, superb restaurant
Price Range:	Moderate to expensive

MENDOCINO HOTEL

Mendocino, California

THE MENDOCINO HOTEL is the only hotel remaining from a time when this was a booming port for the logging trade. The original structure of the hotel, dating from 1878, now contains the lobby bar, dining room, kitchen, and some of the upstairs guest bedrooms. Modern additions include the beautiful Heeser Garden Suites.

In a way, the hotel reflects much of Mendocino's history. Built at a time when the town had a population of twenty thousand, compared to one thousand today, it was known as the Temperance House—"the one good bastion of Christian morals in a town of loggers." Its fortunes then dipped until 1975, when it was bought by R. O. Peterson with the intention of restoring it as authentically as possible.

As a result of this restoration, the property now contains many treasures from around the world. There is a very comfortable lobby lounge, with an open fire; and an excellent dining room featuring period wallpaper and mirrors, original oil paintings, a massive English sideboard, and nineteenth-century glass screens from British railway stations. The food is excellent, too (the hotel has its own bakery).

There is a beautifully carved antique oak bar, set beneath a stained-glass dome, and a carefully tended Victorian garden. The fifty-one bedrooms and suites are all comfortably equipped and have modern plumbing, but some rooms in the older part of the building are very small. Room service is available.

Originally settled principally by New Englanders, the historic village of Mendocino looks like a coastal village in Maine. Pacific storms can fill the fields with fog, to give the surroundings a mysterious and romantic atmosphere. San Francisco is about a three-hour drive away; the region's plentiful wineries and spectacular redwoods are much closer.

THE GHOSTS of the Mendocino Hotel are a series of mysterious figures that appear both in and around the hotel—but nobody can hazard a guess as to their identity. The only clue is that the town of Mendocino is a former fishing village on a particularly treacherous stretch of coast. Many fisherfolk have lost their lives in storms around here, so perhaps some of the victims and their loved ones remain in this otherwise lovely spot.

But the beautiful young woman, who appeared in the lounge and spent some moments gazing out the window before mysteriously disappearing, was no fisherman. Nor is the Victorian woman who haunts Tables 6 and 8 in the restaurant, where she appears in a mirror.

Front desk clerk Dorothy Pear-Green, who witnessed the former strange occurrence, explains:

"One night I had just stepped into the back office when I happened to look through the office window into the lounge. I saw a beautiful woman, with long blonde hair and beautifully dressed, standing in the lounge window gazing out onto the bay.

"She looked like an honest-to-goodness real person. I looked down for a moment to pick up some papers, and when I looked up again she had gone. She certainly wasn't one of our guests: She was dressed in Edwardian style, almost Gibson-girl fashion."

Pear-Green has also heard voices calling "Dottie"—which was her childhood nickname and not known to anyone in the hotel. She says, "I would turn around expecting to see someone, but there was nobody there."

This said, she is quick to emphasize that since starting work at the hotel when it opened nine years ago, "I have had nothing but good experiences here."

The girls who make up the bedrooms, however, have several times reported making up the twin beds in Room 10, then going back with clean towels a few moments later and finding a body-shaped indentation on one of the beds. Dorothy Pear-Green, who slept in Room 10 as an experiment, says she awoke in the night and "felt this presence in the room—a sort of heaviness."

A guest who took a tumble on the empty wooden staircase complained he had felt an unseen presence push him. In Room 307—one of the garden rooms—a boy staying with his mother watched amazed as the mirror began to cloud up and a man's face appeared in it. Mother and son watched the apparition for a full five minutes before the face faded.

But these are isolated incidents to which there were no witnesses. The hotel is an attractive property in a very pretty little town, full of distinctive houses. It takes some time to realize what is different about the skyline. Mendocino has more than its fair share of widows' walks—the rooftop balconies where the recently widowed could take the evening air without interrupting their mourning. It is a reminder that, in its time, Mendocino has been a sad place.

MENDOCINO HOTEL

Address:	45080 Main Street, P.O. Box 587, Mendocino, California 95460
Telephone:	(707) 937-0511 or (800) 548-0513
Facilities:	Excellent restaurant
Price Range:	Moderate

NOYO RIVER LODGE

Fort Bragg, California

NOYO RIVER LODGE is perched on a bluff on a bend at the mouth of the Noyo River and stands in two acres of lushly landscaped grounds. Paths lead down to the busy harbor, where sea lions bark an exuberant welcome to the returning fishing boats.

A twin-gabled house, built for a lumber baron in 1868, the property has been remodeled and completely refurbished to provide comfortable bed-and-breakfast accommodations. But the original craftsmanship of the Norwegian shipbuilders who built the house has been carefully preserved.

The guest rooms and suites are beautiful. They all have private bathrooms, antique decorations, and couches and chairs in which to curl up if the weather is unkind. Many rooms also have fireplaces, cable TV, private decks, even adjoining sun rooms. Feeling lonely? That problem has been solved—for each room has its own resident teddy bear.

Guests are offered a glass of wine and snacks before going off to dine in one of the many restaurants in Fort Bragg. Breakfast is served on the sundecks overlooking the river and Fort Bragg's busy harbor—with the firelit dining room coming into use if it's stormy. Puzzles and board games are provided in the living room, and there is a library of books to borrow. There's a no-smoking rule, and pets cannot be accommodated.

There are lots to see and do in Fort Bragg, a charming little town. Beaches and state parks with hiking trails are practically on the doorstep. The famous Skunk Train ride into the redwoods is a top attraction, as are visits to the Botanical Gardens, museums, antique shops, and art galleries. Visitors can go horseback riding on the beach, while boats set off for fishing expeditions and whale-watching excursions from the docks just below Noyo River Lodge.

THE GHOST—or, rather, the ghosts—at the Noyo River Lodge are a honeymoon couple who stayed in Room 5 in the 1940s. One evening after dinner, they set off for a drive up the coast—the man wearing distinctive light-colored clothing and his blonde bride in a red dress. They never came back, for they were both killed in an automobile accident near Grange Hall.

But in 1983, perhaps the young couple *did* return to the hotel where they had been so happy. The former owner, who was showing another couple around the hotel one day, was surprised when a young man wearing distinctive light-colored slacks and shirt and a girl in a red dress—both of them looking very pale—emerged from Room 5 and walked past the visitors on the landing and down the stairs. When he had finished showing the visitors around, and because he had not seen the other couple before, the former owner asked the restaurant manager, who had been standing at the foot of the stairs, where the two strangers had gone. But the restaurant manager insisted that no one had come down the stairs, and a check on the guest register showed Room 5 was empty.

The previous owner, who has since died, also reported disturbances involving Rooms 1 and 3. Doors opened and closed mysteriously. A human form sometimes appeared on freshly made beds. Once as he left the empty hotel, he also saw a girl in a white dress parting the curtains in Room 3 and staring down at him. When he went back inside the hotel to check, he found Room 3 deserted. But, on what was a very warm day, the room felt bitterly cold.

NOYO RIVER LODGE

It seems as if the Noyo River Lodge's ghosts play tag around the second-floor bedrooms. Room 5 is not the honeymoon suite and there are no stories to explain the girl in Room 3 or the phantom sleepers in Rooms 1 and 3. The hotel had recently changed hands at the time this book was being researched, and the new manager had not experienced anything out of the ordinary. But she did let me browse through the visitors' journals kept in each room which tell the recent history of the hotel through guests' eyes.

Part of Room 3's journal was missing—allegedly destroyed by a guest who found a "frightening" story in it. And Room 5's journal recorded that, in 1988, a couple known only as Fred and Carol were moving to Room 4 "because of circumstances beyond our control." Mysteriously, they had made no entry in Room 4's journal, so that's where their story stopped. Could they have been a man in light-colored clothing and a blonde girl in a red dress?

NOYO RIVER LODGE

Address:	500 Casa del Noyo, Fort Bragg, California 95437
Telephone:	(707) 964-8045 or (800) 628-1126
Facilities:	Beautiful bedrooms, harbor views, and excursions
Price Range:	Inexpensive to moderate

HOTEL QUEEN MARY
Long Beach, California

ONCE, SHE WAS the most famous oceangoing liner in the world. Now she is a unique hotel berthed permanently in Long Beach Harbor. And, even if she will never sail the seven seas again, the giant RMS *Queen Mary* is maintaining her sixty-year tradition of entertaining guests in comfort and style as she fulfills her new role as the Hotel Queen Mary.

The *Queen Mary* made her maiden voyage in 1936 and spent thirty-one years at sea. During that time she made 1,001 Atlantic crossings, logged more than three million miles, saw war service as a troopship, and carried more than two million passengers. Now included in the *National Register of Historic Places*, she is the centerpiece of the Queen Mary Seaport attraction and, with her large, elegant staterooms and numerous restaurants and banquet rooms, a top-class hotel.

The 365 bedrooms were once the liner's first-class staterooms, and, although they are not as large as modern hotel bedrooms, they are full of customized woodwork and veneers, and plenty of 1930s-style art deco furniture. More recent additions to the staterooms are color TV, touch-tone telephones, and central heating and air conditioning.

Award-winning dining is just footsteps away at Sir Winston's, which offers fine continental cuisine for luncheon or dinner, or at the Chelsea Restaurant on the Promenade Deck, which serves only dinner and specializes in seafood. A champagne Sunday brunch is served

HOTEL QUEEN MARY

in the Grand Salon, while breakfast and other informal meals may be taken in the Promenade Cafe.

There is live entertainment on board in the art deco Observation Bar, a favorite meeting place for San Diego society. There are also fast-food outlets, boutiques, and souvenir shops on board the vast ship. To find your way around you can join one of the daily guided tours.

THE GHOSTS on board the *Queen Mary* are numerous and are backed up by plenty of eyewitness accounts.

"Sightings, voices, and noises have been reported time and time again," hotel management admits. "You can ask almost any engineer, painter, security officer, or alleyway worker if they've had an unusual or unexplained experience, and they will oblige with a story."

There's the security man, for example, who had to patrol the ship at night when it was undergoing conversion. His guard dog refused to pass through watertight Door 13 in Shaft Alley. A check of the records showed an eighteen-year-old crewman had been crushed to death at that spot during a drill in 1966. Guests touring the ship have since seen a pale youth in naval uniform passing through Door 13.

Or how about the tour guide who, walking through the engine room at the end of the day, saw a bearded man in blue overalls coming up behind her. Knowing he wasn't on the staff, she waited to guide him to the exit. But before he reached her, he vanished.

One particularly haunted spot is the first-class pool, maybe the spookiest part of the ship. Tour guides have seen both a swimmer in a 1930s costume and a woman in 1960s clothing in the pool area, but both disappeared before they could be questioned. Security guards often hear voices and the sound of splashing coming from the pool; when they enter they find it deserted. Particularly puzzling is the fact that the unseen revelers often leave wet footprints on the floor. The pool is kept empty.

The kitchens, the original third-class children's playroom (a toddler died there in 1946 and the sound of a child crying can still be heard), a couple of first-class suites, and the forward storage area are all said to be haunted. And who is the lovely woman, dressed in a simple white evening gown, who is dancing by herself in the shadows in the Queen's Saloon?

During the war, the *Queen Mary* served as a troopship. Repainted and christened the gray ghost, she was fast enough and powerful enough to outpace any German warship. With Hitler putting a huge price on her head, she had orders to stop for nothing. One day, performing a complicated zigzag pattern at sea, she sliced the British light cruiser *Curacoa* in half and, because she could not stop to pick them up, 338 of the *Curacoa's* crew drowned. One of the gray ghost's oddest ghost stories concerns that incident.

A TV crew filming on the ship very recently left their audio equipment running overnight in the part of the ship known as the Bosun's Locker. Next day they heard on the tape the sound of a terrible collision at sea and poundings on the hull. The *Queen Mary*, moored forever to her Long Beach dock, had not moved. But once again, she had undergone that dreadful accident at sea, still the blackest spot in her proud history.

HOTEL QUEEN MARY

Address:	1126 Queen's Highway, Long Beach, California 90802-6390
Telephone:	(310) 435-3511; for stateroom reservations (310) 432-6964 or (800) 437-2934
Facilities:	Full luxury hotel facilities in a historic art deco shipboard setting
Price Range:	Moderate

RADISSON HOLLYWOOD ROOSEVELT HOTEL

Hollywood, California

SITUATED RIGHT in the heart of Hollywood, the Radisson Hollywood Roosevelt Hotel is a stylish property built in 1927 as the centerpiece of the film world—a role it still fulfills. Always *the* place to see and be seen, it staged the first-ever Academy Awards ceremony in its Blossom Ballroom in 1929, and it has hosted a variety of major movie premieres and opening night galas during the following four decades.

Then in 1983, the hotel—named after President Theodore Roosevelt—began a two-year, forty-million-dollar restoration. Original features such as the classic Spanish revival style exterior and the famous Blossom Room remained as they had always been. Hand-painted ceilings were restored; Spanish wrought-iron grilles were renovated. Finally, in March 1986, her dignity regained, the hotel was declared open again at a gala ceremony attended by fifteen hundred of Hollywood's rich and famous.

Today the hotel features 335 beautifully appointed rooms, including twenty luxury suites. Among the suites are a Grand Suite, the Celebrity Suite, ten movie-themed suites, and nine three-room Hollywood suites. There are also sixty-five cabana rooms in a tropical garden setting bordering an Olympic-sized heated swimming pool, Jacuzzi, and the Tropicana Bar.

The hotel restaurant, Theodore's, offers fine dining in the California/continental style. It's open for breakfast, lunch, and dinner seven days a week and serves an elaborate champagne brunch on Sundays. The cabaret nightclub, Cinegrill, hosts top-name entertainers. Cover charges and show times vary.

Hollywood's "Walk of Fame," where the big movie entertainers of the past and the present have their names engraved in stars on the sidewalk, is right outside the hotel on Hollywood Boulevard. The renowned Mann's Chinese Theater is also on the doorstep, and attractions such as Universal Studios, Disneyland, Beverly Hills, and the Hollywood Bowl are all within easy reach.

THE GHOST at the Radisson Hollywood Roosevelt Hotel is Marilyn Monroe. She's joined there by Montgomery Clift and a number of other stars.

The renovation of the property seemed to disturb all sorts of spirits. Even the hotel's publicity material admits, "Yes, this property is haunted. There are many ghosts and spirits we know about, and probably a lot more that we don't know."

The easiest to check out is in the Blossom Ballroom. In mid-December 1985, just two weeks before the hotel's unofficial reopening, actor Alan Russell, working as personal assistant to the general manager, discovered a cool spot in the ballroom. Lots of staff and guests have experienced it, and it has even been investigated scientifically. It's a circle, about thirty inches in diameter. The temperature in the circle is about ten degrees cooler than the rest of the room. There is no obvious explanation for this and, although the cool spot dissipates when the room is crowded, it soon returns when the room is empty. Psychics say there is a man in black there, showing a lot of anxiety.

Cleaner Suzanne Leonard had plenty of cause for anxiety herself on the same day Alan Russell discovered the cool spot. She was dusting the tall, dark-framed mirror in the general manager's office when she saw the reflection of a blonde girl in the glass. She turned around to speak to her, but there was no one there. Puzzled, Leonard reported the incident to her boss, who revealed that the mirror had once belonged to Marilyn Monroe and had been removed from the poolside suite Marilyn occupied at the hotel when the film star died. The mirror has now been moved to the lower level elevator landing, so curious guests can keep their own lookout for Marilyn's ghost.

Stay at the hotel long enough and you could even cast your own film. Montgomery Clift, who spent three months in Room 928 while filming *From Here to Eternity*, has been felt brushing past people in the corridor outside the room where he once paced for hours, learning his lines. There's a "ghost writer" in the personnel office, who taps away at the electric typewriter after the empty office is locked up for the night; a lighting man who turns the lights on and off in Star Suite 1101/1102; and a sound man who makes telephone calls to the switchboard from empty rooms. There are even cast parties. Guests quite often call to complain about noisy neighbors in the room next door to theirs, only to be told the room is empty.

It would all make a thrilling film. But Montgomery Clift does not seem to welcome modern filmmakers to Room 928 and has caused all kinds of problems. Marilyn's mirror doesn't want to be filmed, and the cool spot in the ballroom is cold enough to affect audio equipment.

Research psychic Peter James spent some time investigating the hotel's phenomena in the spring of 1992. He felt the presence of numerous film stars: Carmen Miranda in a hallway on the third floor; Humphrey Bogart near the elevator; Errol Flynn, Edward Arnold, and Betty Grable in the Blossom Room; and Montgomery Clift up in Room 928. As he walked into the Tropicana Bar, James exclaimed, "Marilyn Monroe is here, right here, and her presence is very strong."

So who needs to go to the movies? It's all there in the Hollywood Roosevelt Hotel, the stuff of which a publicity man's dreams are made. And, quite coincidentally, the hotel has felt moved to put out an eight-page press release detailing its phantom film stars and their latest personal appearances.

RADISSON HOLLYWOOD ROOSEVELT HOTEL

Address:	7000 Hollywood Boulevard, Hollywood, California 90028
Telephone:	(213) 466-7000, or for reservations (800) 833-3333
Fax:	(213) 462-8056
Facilities:	Full modern hotel facilities, including Olympic-size pool, Hollywood memorabilia gallery, restaurant, and cabaret nightclub
Price Range:	Expensive

SAN REMO HOTEL

San Francisco, California

A CHEAP ROOM can be hard to find in San Francisco, so the historic San Remo Hotel—constructed in 1906 in the Fisherman's Wharf and North Beach area and recently restored—has a welcome spot on the tourist map.

A family-owned and operated property, the San Remo Inn is very like a European-style *pension*. It was once a boardinghouse for dock workers displaced by the San Francisco fire, and it has a lot of rooms—sixty-two of them—packed into its three stories. The rooms are small, the walls thin, the bathrooms shared, and the corridors narrow—but that doesn't mean the owners have not done their best with the space available.

On the contrary, the rooms are nicely furnished with brass beds, antiques and wickerwork, and have ceiling fans. Ask for Room 42 or Room 43: they overlook Mason Street. The corridors are full of plants and interesting knickknacks. There is a lovely little penthouse on the roof. It doesn't look like much from the outside, but it does have its own facilities, glorious views, and a price tag within the "inexpensive" bracket.

Sadly, the hotel does not serve breakfast. Guests have to make do with the hot drinks and confectionery from vending machines in the snackery. The adjoining restaurant was closed, possibly in the process of changing hands, when I was there.

But the San Remo does have its own piano bar and cocktail lounge, it is clean and comfortable, the staff is friendly, and it's doing its best. For the young, or travelers on a budget, it is probably the biggest bargain in town, convenient to some of the city's leading attractions, from Fisherman's Wharf and the cable car turnaround to Golden Gate Bridge.

THE GHOST at the San Remo Hotel is said to be that of a long-term guest who, toward the end of the "flower power" era, worked as a madam in San Francisco's once-famous red-light district. She died in her tiny room in the southern part of the hotel around 1980 and her body was not found for several days.

When her remains were taken away for burial, her spirit stayed on in the hotel. Or so some staff members and guests believe.

"I'm not psychic, but there is someone here," front desk manager Teresa Quinn says. "Sometimes, when I work here alone late at night, the lights go on and off by themselves.

"The last time that happened I called out, 'Is there anybody there?' but there was no reply and nobody appeared. I'm not scared. I don't think anybody is. And this is a nice place to work."

Another happy employee is Minako Ohara who says, prosaically, "I haven't seen anything." Ohara admits, however, that working alone in the office late at night can be a spooky experience because the old clapboard building sometimes creaks and groans alarmingly. She never feels frightened, though, because, "if there is a ghost here, it's a nice one."

SAN REMO HOTEL

Address:	2247 Mason Street, San Francisco, California 94133
Telephone:	(415) 776-8688 or (800) 352-REMO
Fax:	(415) 776-2811
Facilities:	Central situation, adjoining restaurant
Price Range:	Inexpensive

SCOTIA INN

Scotia, California

LOCATED AT THE northern end of the Avenue of the Giants, where northern California's redwood trees seem to scrape the sky, the Scotia Inn is the original hotel for the town of Scotia—once owned in its entirety by the Pacific Lumber Company and one of the last remaining company towns in the United States.

The old hotel was torn down in 1923 and replaced with the present, more elegant building. Extensively renovated in 1985, the hotel now aims to bring back the era of the 1920s. All the rooms have been decorated with fine printed wallpaper, filled with antiques, and equipped with clawfoot baths. The bridal suite has a private hot tub, and the staff will serve champagne in any room. No wonder the hotel brochure warns that reservations are always advisable.

The pampering extends to the dining room, with its sparkling chandeliers, vases of fresh flowers, and walls covered with paintings by local artists. The furniture is polished redwood and the menu is extensive. The hotel has earned a reputation as a good place to dine.

There is also a family-style lounge, large-screen TV, and games. This, along with the inn's banqueting facilities, has helped make Scotia Inn a firm favorite with the locals, who tend to use it as a home away from home.

Eureka is about a thirty-minute drive to the north, and San Francisco about five hours to the south. But the redwoods and varied wildlife are the main attraction. Locals will tell you to go hug a tree; it's supposed to be therapeutic. But, in these parts, you'll need a long reach.

THE GHOST at the Scotia Inn is called Frank. At least, that's what managers Jerry and Hillary Carley call him. Hillary Carley says, "He is very mischievous. He slams doors and turns lights off and on. He likes to scare people, but he is harmless. Just devilish.

"He follows women into the bathroom, then disappears when they get scared. He also gets people to follow him, thinking he is someone else, then disappears."

The Carleys believe their phantom prankster is the ghost of a man who committed suicide at the inn back in the 1950s. Be that as it may, the Carleys also have a much more mysterious tale to tell.

About six years ago, when they were selling their house in Eureka and moving to Scotia, their new home was not quite ready so they stayed in the inn. Their daughter was about eighteen months old at the time, and very active.

So Hillary Carley was alarmed to be awakened one night at about 3:00 A.M. by the sound of "a little girl, laughing and running down the hall in the hotel." Thinking she was their own daughter who had somehow clambered out of her cot, the Carleys checked, but found her still safely tucked up in bed, fast asleep.

Next morning they asked the manager if the child they'd heard in the hall was all right and discovered that their daughter was the only child staying in the inn. Hillary Carley reports, "Many people have heard this little girl many times, running merrily through the inn."

Curious, the Carleys have tried to find out who the child is. But local residents could offer no clue. Then one recent day, a retired doctor told them that many years ago, long before the freeway was built, there was a road bridge outside the inn. One tragic day, he recalled, a speeding car had struck and killed a little girl who was laughing as she ran across the bridge.

SCOTIA INN

Address:	Main and Mill Streets, P.O. Box 248, Scotia, California 95565
Telephone:	(707) 764-5683
Facilities:	In-house restaurant and pub
Price Range:	Inexpensive to moderate

U. S. GRANT HOTEL

San Diego, California

WHEN IT WAS opened in 1910, it was hailed by the press as one of the premier grand hotels in the United States. And it still is. Exquisitely restored, the U. S. Grant Hotel, built in honor of the Civil War hero and eighteenth president of the United States, Ulysses S. Grant, is now registered as a National Historic Site.

The 280 guest rooms, including fifty suites, are all presented in turn-of-the-century elegance—with two-poster beds, mahogany furnishings, armoires, and wingback chairs. They all have large bathrooms with marble and ceramic tile tubs. The suites offer built-in bars,

U. S. GRANT HOTEL

fireplaces, chandeliers, and Jacuzzi bathtubs, with views of the down-town skyline and San Diego Bay.

Recent innovations include the business-oriented President's Club-level rooms; and a "pampered pet" program for the dogs and cats guests can't bear to leave at home. Only pets weighing up to fifty pounds are accepted, and this free service is subject to availability. But the pets are as pampered as the paying guests: grooming, dog walk-ing, and even a "turn-down" bedtime biscuit in place of the ubiqui-tous chocolate mint on the pillow.

The award-winning Grant Grill is the hotel's top restaurant, among America's top ten. There is less formal eating in the entertainment-packed Grant Grill Lounge, and the huge lobby sometimes doubles as a ballroom or a setting for parties. There is round-the-clock room service.

The hotel has its own fitness center, although it can also make arrangements for guests to use a nearby athletic club. It is situated on the doorstep of San Diego's Gaslamp Quarter, right opposite the Horton Plaza shopping mall. San Diego Bay, the city's convention center, and tourist attractions such as Sea World and the famous San Diego Zoo are all within easy reach.

THE GHOST at the U. S. Grant Hotel is Fannie Josephine Chaffee Grant, the first wife of Ulysses S. Grant Jr., who haunts a function room known as the Crystal Room.

Grant Jr.—known as "Buck"—and Fannie Chaffee were married in New York in 1880. Four years later, after the family had lost all their money in a scandalous brokerage firm failure, the Grants moved to San Diego. Fannie was having health problems.

They prospered in their new home. Grant became an assistant district attorney and his wife, whose family had made money from mining, land, and banking in Colorado, bought San Diego's first luxury hotel, the Horton House, in 1895. Ten years later the old hotel was demolished to make way for construction of the U. S. Grant Hotel, which Grant planned as a homage to his late father.

But in 1909, before the new hotel was opened, Fannie died. Since then, her spirit appears to have lingered on in the Crystal Room. She has been seen by employees, guests, and even (so rumor has it) by a detachment of Secret Service personnel stationed at the hotel during the 1992 presidential election campaign.

One mystery is what connection Fannie has with the Crystal Room. It was incomplete at the time of her death. But hotel spokesperson Robin Maydeck says, "Sightings of her—clothed in turn-of-the-century garb, sometimes white, sometimes black—strolling near and in the Crystal Room, or sitting in the Crystal Room smoking a cigarette, have been reported by the guests and personnel."

Maydeck adds that Fannie likes to rattle the room's crystal chandeliers. But she is anxious to emphasize that "Fannie Grant is a very benign spirit and not constant in her attentions to the Crystal Room. There are no stories of the spirit threatening a person in any way."

At least one fellow employee is not quite as confident as Maydeck. She prefers to remain anonymous but said she had undergone several strange experiences in the Crystal Room: unexplained colors on the wall sconces, the room icy cold on a warm day. In a nearby room, she has experienced "a presence you can almost, but not quite, hear."

U. S. GRANT HOTEL

Address:	236 Broadway, San Diego, California 92101
Telephone:	(619) 232-3121, or for reservations (800) HERITAGE
Fax:	(619) 232-3626
Facilities:	Elegant furnishings, special business floors, "pampered pet" program
Price Range:	Expensive, but ask about special packages

VINEYARD HOUSE

Coloma, California

VINEYARD HOUSE, which served as everything from winery to jail during the boom-and-bust years of the California gold rush, is still the center of activity in El Dorado County, right at the heart of the region where gold was discovered by James Marshall at Sutter's Mill in Coloma.

The ruins of the old winery are now part of historic Gold Discovery Park, just a few yards behind the Vineyard House. This bed-and-breakfast accommodation and restaurant has a historic feel about it, too. It is furnished in period style, but retains a slightly spartan atmosphere.

There are seven bedrooms, all decorated in a different style to match the gold-rush-era characters after whom they are named. All but one have shared bathrooms. Guests are welcomed during the afternoon with wine and cheese. Country-style breakfasts are taken either in the dining room or on the veranda.

The restaurant, consisting of five period-furnished dining rooms, is well known locally for its home-cooked country fare. Dishes are inventive and the helpings are huge. How does braised rabbit with roast garlic mashed potatoes sound? And if the answer to that is "thirsty work," there is a huge, very popular basement cellar bar known as the Saloon—a former wine cellar with walls of solid granite.

THE GHOST at the Vineyard House is Robert Chalmers, who built the inn with his wife, Louisa, in 1878. He is often spotted in the cellar bar of the hotel. Louisa has been seen walking across the road from the Pioneer Cemetery opposite the hotel, where she and her husband are buried.

Robert was a forty-niner, one of the countless prospectors who flocked to California when gold was discovered at Sutter's Mill in 1849. The population of Coloma, presently 175, exploded to around twenty thousand. Among the gold diggers seeking quick riches were Robert and his partner, Martin Alhoff. But they found prospecting hard, tedious, and unrewarding, and in 1852 they tired of the adventure and returned home to Ohio, where Alhoff wooed and wed the fourteen-year-old Louisa Weaver.

The trio returned to Coloma, and Alhoff purchased the land where the Vineyard House now stands and planted, yes, a vineyard. Chalmers built and ran a hotel. Alhoff's Coloma Cellars became the most famous winery in northern California, winning prizes all over the state, but his success was short-lived. He was accused of avoiding state liquor taxes and committed suicide. Chalmers, a dashing ladies' man—and perhaps still a "gold digger"—promptly wed his former partner's wealthy widow, and the couple built the Vineyard House to double as their private mansion and the social center of the area.

It was a glittering time. Chalmers became a state senator, and the famous guests who visited his home included former President Ulysses S. Grant—to whom Chalmers bore a remarkable resemblance. But, once again, success and riches were to be transitory, for Chalmers (possibly suffering from syphilis) began to go mad. Eventually he became so paranoid and violent that he had to be kept chained in the cellar for his own safety. The couple's fortune disappeared. When Chalmers died, Louisa had to mortgage the house and lost it.

But both she and her second husband, it seems, stay on in spirit. Many guests have seen either Robert or Louisa. And there are even reports of a third ghost, the spirit of a child.

Present owners Les and Christine Widger saw a figure standing in the window of Room 3 when they drove up to the (empty) inn;

Room 5 is said to be haunted; and both Room 1 (Louisa's old room) and Room 2 (which was Robert's) are very atmospheric. A photograph taken by a guest of the hotel some years ago showed a shadowy female figure perched precariously on the roof—at the top of a ladder that had no rungs. (The photo is currently on display in the dining room.)

Despite the mysterious episode of the figure in the window, the Widgers don't claim to have seen a ghost themselves. Les Widger allows, "I think there is a lot of energy in this house." Guests, however, are adamant they have seen Robert in both the restaurant and the cellar bar; and on one occasion two people in the bar, neither of whom knew each other or the ghost stories, saw a gray, bearded figure, dressed in a black suit and looking rather like Ulysses S. Grant, materialize in the bar behind a group of drinkers, walk towards a solid brick wall, then disappear.

Curious, Widger arranged to spend the night alone in the bar, which in its time served both as the Chalmers' wine cellar and as the local jail. "I am an adventurous fellow," admits the brave Widger. But his curiosity was not to be satisfied, for the night was uneventful. Now Widger sees the spectral Chalmers as a possible useful addition to his staff and says, "If I do see him, I'll give him some work to do."

Waiting tables perhaps? Waitresses at the inn claim the Chalmers' baby son, George, who died when he was six years old, haunts the house, too.

Rather more convincing is the testament of a group of local police officers who held a party in the Vineyard House. Three or four of them sat up in the parlor until 3:00 A.M., keeping an eye half open for the ghosts. Then they heard the sound of talking, laughing, and merriment coming from Rooms 2 and 6. Thinking their colleagues were continuing to party without them, the officers went upstairs and opened the doors of Rooms 2 and 6. They were quite empty.

VINEYARD HOUSE

Address:	P.O. Box 517, 530 Cold Springs Road, Coloma, California 95613
Telephone:	(916) 622-2217
Facilities:	Historic setting, cellar bar
Price Range:	Inexpensive to moderate

MAPLE HILL FARM

Coventry, Connecticut

MAPLE HILL FARM was built in 1731, when Nathaniel Woodward settled a 175-acre plot in North Coventry. He set about putting up a house to serve as a comfortable family home and to impress the neighbors. That same building still stands today as a monument to the ingenuity of colonial builders. Their use of stone, oak, and chestnut has helped the present owners offer guests a bed-and-breakfast in a welcoming atmosphere, comfortable and convenient.

The four guest rooms are large, quiet, and furnished with antiques. But this is also a home away from home. Guests are encouraged to walk in the seven acres of gardens, talk to the horses, swim in the pool on the grounds, or just relax in a hammock under the maple tree. There is also a screened porch for lounging, and roaring fires in winter. Want to get fit? A hot tub in a flower-filled solarium, a well-equipped exercise area, and bicycles allow guests to exercise daily.

A full country breakfast is served on heirloom china. Fresh fruit and pastries complement a menu which includes eggs from the farm's own free-range chickens. This appetizing fare is, says this bed-and-breakfast's brochure, "accompanied by lively conversation and classical music."

Although breakfast is the only meal offered, there are several fine restaurants within only a few minutes' drive, so Maple Hill Farm is suitable for longer stays. A nonsmoking policy is in operation.

The farm is only ten minutes away from the University of Connecticut campus, and downtown Hartford is reached in about half an hour. The tourist attractions of eastern Connecticut are also within easy reach, and there are two eighteen-hole golf courses nearby.

THE GHOST at Maple Hill Farm is Maude, the last member of the original family that built the house to actually live there.

Innkeepers Tony Felice and MaryBeth Gorke-Felice don't like the word "haunting," because they feel it might have negative connotations. As MaryBeth Gorke-Felice says, "The events have never been unpleasant, unkind, or in any way 'negative.' But how else does one describe encounters with spirits, if not as 'haunting'?"

The couple moved into the farm in 1981 with their five children and dog. One of the first friends they made was a local man named Wilfred, who had been raised in the house. Over the years, Wilfred has given them many old photos of his family and of the property.

To begin with, the Felices were kept busy by the demands of their large family. When their daughters said, on several occasions, they had heard someone in the house, the entire family would organize frenetic "search parties" only to find nothing. When the Felices' son said he'd seen a white-clad figure drift past his bedroom door, they thought he was just trying to frighten his sisters.

It was a family vacation which first brought Maude into the limelight. With farm animals, a greenhouse, and the dog all needing to be looked after, they got friends to move in as house-sitters. They, too, heard someone moving around upstairs. They, their son, and even the dog, twice heard someone walking from room to room. But, once again, searches of the house were fruitless.

When the house-sitters told their story to the Felices, it was the first time the couple had seriously considered that "someone else might be in the house with us." Soon afterward, MaryBeth Gorke-Felice came face-to-face with Maude.

"I was returning dishes to the cupboard in the dining room, and I saw a lady in gauzy white passing from that room into the downstairs bedroom," she says. "She looked very much like the picture of Wilfred's mother, Maude. That's how we came to call her Maude."

Research showed that Maude had been born in the house, grown up there, married in the front parlor, had eight children, and then suddenly died in her fifties. The spot where she died—the downstairs bedroom.

"We feel she was not ready to leave, and has been 'keeping tabs' on the house since," MaryBeth Gorke-Felice says.

Maude certainly keeps tabs on any work being done in the house. She once stood silently in front of a plasterer, who was restoring an old fireplace in the hall, and made him feel so nervous that he explained, "I'm just repairing this wall." At that, the woman vanished. She has also appeared to at least a couple of guests. One woman guest, who was frightened when she awoke and saw the phantom figure, claims that Maude said to her, "Everything is all right; you can go back to sleep."

Felice and his wife do not alert guests to Maude's presence. That makes the stories and the similarities between them all the more convincing. The couple told me, "People have offered to exorcise Maude. But we feel this is her home, and she will probably be here long after we are gone. So we say 'no thank-you.' Maude is the ongoing 'lady of the house.' "

MAPLE HILL FARM

Address:	365 Goose Lane, Coventry, Connecticut 06238
Telephone:	(203) 742-0635 or (800) 742-0635
Facilities:	Charming country bed-and-breakfast with a modern touch
Price Range:	Inexpensive

DON CESAR BEACH RESORT

St. Petersburg Beach, Florida

FLORIDA'S FAMOUS "pink palace" has towered over St. Petersburg Beach on the beautiful and still relatively uncrowded Gulf Coast since 1928. Known to its regular clients simply as "the Don," the Don CeSar Beach Resort has recently completed a multimillion-dollar renovation (the hotel prefers to call it a "revitalization") to ensure it retains its place as one of the leading holiday hotels in America.

F. Scott Fitzgerald, who was prepared to put his love for the Don on paper, referred to it as "the hotel in an island wilderness." St. Petersburg Beach has grown a bit since then—but it hasn't produced anything to match its most famous and most easily recognizable building.

Whatever you want on holiday, the Don probably has it. The 277 guest rooms all have modern facilities but maintain the classic style that has become the hotel's hallmark, the colorful flowered bedspreads and draperies complementing light washed woods with shell motifs.

The lobby area has been redesigned, and the adjoining lobby lounge is in "grand old living-room" country-house style. Other public rooms include the Sea Porch Cafe Restaurant and Sunset Bar and Lounge, an ice-cream parlor, the King Charles Ballroom (where the hotel serves its famous Sunday brunch), and a new signature restaurant, the Maritana Grille, which specializes in Floribbean cuisine. As this is first and foremost a holiday hotel, jackets are not required, even in the Maritana Grille.

Outside facilities have been "revitalized" to match the sparkling interior of the wedding-cake hotel. Two swimming pools (one of them featuring underwater stereo sound) are surrounded by the multilevel boardwalk, and the new beach club and spa encourages personal fitness without too much in the way of strenuous activity.

The vast beach of white sand is right behind the hotel, and guided ecological walks along the shore are recommended. There's golf on the Isla del Sol. Other nearby attractions include the magnificent Salvador Dali Museum in St. Petersburg and the famous Busch Gardens. Day trips take in the rest of central Florida's famous family attractions.

THE GHOST at the Don CeSar is Thomas Rowe, who built the property in 1928 as a tribute to his true love, Lucinda, a Spanish opera singer. Some people say Lucinda can be seen there, too.

Rowe had always promised Lucinda they would run away together and he would build her a pink Spanish castle with towers and rooftop balcony overlooking the sea. He kept his promise but sadly, Lucinda did not live to see it. Forbidden by her parents from continuing her association with Rowe after they met in London in the mid-1890s, she was taken back to Spain and the lovers never saw one another again.

Rowe's letters to the dark-eyed, raven-haired Lucinda were always returned unopened. Then one day a newspaper clipping announcing Lucinda's death was sent to Rowe at his home in New York, along with a final letter from his lover, asking him to forgive her parents. It reads, "We found each other before, and shall again. Time is infinite. I wait for you by our fountain to share our timeless love."

The letter—addressed to Rowe as "my beloved Don Cesar" (after the character in Wallace's light opera *Maritana*)—was signed "Maritana" (the role Lucinda had sung in London).

Shortly after this, Rowe moved to Florida on medical advice, and he began to build the pink palace he had promised Lucinda. The hotel took three years to build and, at $1.2 million, cost three times more than expected, largely because Rowe insisted that the lobby fountain be a replica of the one in the courtyard where he and Lucinda used to meet.

Rowe, famous for his light summer suits and panama hat, became a familiar local figure. But his hotel was not an immediate success. After Rowe collapsed and died of a heart attack in his beloved lobby in 1940, the property was drafted into duty as a World War II hospital.

It was not until 1972 that work began on renovating the property back into a luxury hotel. The work seemed to disturb the spirit of Rowe, for a panama-hatted figure was seen by construction workers in the lobby and in the corridors on the fifth floor where Rowe had once lived. Soon, hotel staff started seeing the figure, too.

Can you make a deal with a ghost? Yes, according to public relations adviser Lynn Peterson. Commenting on the fact that the phantom figure vanished abruptly from the hotel, Peterson says, "One explanation involves the new owner of the hotel and a bargain he made with Rowe. One evening, the owner claims he came face-to-face with Rowe in the hotel kitchen. The owner explained he felt rumors of the hotel having a ghost would be detrimental to the Don CeSar's success. Some curiosity seekers would love it, but for the majority of people a resident ghost would be unnerving.

"Rowe did not want to leave. The owner offered an alternative. He would decorate four rooms with furnishings of the twenties and thirties era for Rowe and asked that if he materialized at the hotel, he should do so in this area and not in front of the guests or employees."

The panama-hatted phantom liked this offer. The ghost hasn't been seen inside the hotel for more than twenty years. On the other hand, staff and guests alike frequently report they have seen a man in a light-colored suit and a panama hat strolling the grounds. And he has always been accompanied by a young woman with long dark hair and wearing a Spanish peasant's gown.

Perhaps Thomas Rowe and Lucinda have met one another once again by the fountain and walked out into the sunset together to find a timeless love.

Don CeSar Beach Resort

Address:	3400 Gulf Boulevard, St. Petersburg Beach, Florida 33706
Telephone:	(813) 360-1881, or for information (800) 637-7200, or hotel direct (800) 282-1116
Fax:	(813) 367-6952
Facilities:	Beachfront property with international reputation and full resort facilities
Price Range:	Expensive (but look for special offers)

HERLONG MANSION

Micanopy, Florida

ACCORDING TO *Florida Trend* magazine, Micanopy is the prettiest town in Florida. It is "just oak and pecan trees draped with Spanish moss that shade a sleepy two-lane road to Old Florida's last stand." And the crown jewel in this pollution-free paragon of a place? The Herlong Mansion, says the magazine.

It is hard to disagree with that verdict. Begun in 1875 as a humble two-story house, the property grew along with the Herlong family's fortunes from timber and citrus. By 1915, times were good enough to build a classical revival mansion on top of the original structure, complete with a Corinthian-columned frontage, and leaded glass and mahogany inlays galore.

Kim and Simone Evans moved to Micanopy from a Disney hotel in Orlando in 1987 and turned the slightly dilapidated mansion into an inn. It now belongs to Sonny Howard, who runs what *Florida Trend* describes as "easily Florida's most elegant bed-and-breakfast." There are eleven rooms and suites in all, with private facilities. Prices vary according to the accommodation. The rooms are all equipped with fireplaces and are furnished with fine antiques. Smoking is prohibited.

Prices include a full breakfast of homemade pastries, croissants, eggs, sausage, and fresh fruit.

Micanopy is a quiet and romantic little place, its tree-canopied streets full of antique and curio shops (there were sixteen of them at the last count). There is not a fast-food outlet to be seen. The Micanopy Museum, housed in the one-hundred-year-old Thrasher Warehouse, is within walking distance of the Herlong Mansion. It is a short drive to Cross Creek and the home of Marjorie Kinnan Rawlings, the Pulitzer Prize-winning author of *The Yearling*; or to the twenty-thousand-acre wildlife sanctuary of Payne's Prairie State Preserve. The family attractions of Orlando are about a two-hour drive away.

HERLONG MANSION

THE GHOST at the Herlong Mansion is Inez Herlong, the former owner of the house, who so loved the property that she sacrificed her family ties to do so.

The first people to "meet" Inez were a team of workmen brought in to strip and varnish the floors in 1987. Because there was no electricity in the house, the crew slept in sleeping bags in the ground-floor parlor. Sometime between midnight and dawn they heard the door of a second-floor room open and close, followed by the sound of footsteps in the hall. Suspecting local hooligans, the workmen ran up to the hall—only to find it deserted.

Innkeeper Sonny Howard believes the spirit the workmen heard was Inez, because she braved a lifelong family feud to own the house. Her mother left the property to be divided among her six children, but they quarreled about who should live there. Eventually, Inez Herlong Miller, who had also inherited money from her husband's estate, bought out her brothers and sisters after a two-year legal battle. She had won her beloved home, but she lost her family. None of them ever spoke to her again.

In her declining years, Inez was increasingly unable to look after the house properly. She collapsed and died while cleaning and polishing on the second floor. When her remains left the building, however, her spirit stayed on. She now helps Sonny Howard "run" the inn, and Howard takes delight in telling his guests the story of the Herlong Mansion's ghost.

But he doesn't tell them the story until after breakfast. And then only when he has asked everyone whether they slept well.

"I'm a logical man," he says, "but 75 percent of all the 'experiences' revealed at the breakfast table, in the broad light of day, come from people who slept (or didn't sleep) in Inez's favorite room."

Which room is that? Howard is not saying, not until *you* have spent the night there. This book is not saying, either. But guests who have been in the haunted room report locked doors opening, lights flickering on and off, lowered window shades being raised, and "a feeling" of Inez's presence.

If you are shy about admitting your experiences in public over breakfast, Howard keeps a scrapbook. In it there is a letter from one man who wrote, "When we turned in for the night, Nancy was reading and I was trying to sleep. I rolled over and opened my eyes. There in the mirror over the dressing-table was an apparition floating across the room. It couldn't be seen in the room itself, only in the mirror. It had a red shawl, or hood, over its head and although I couldn't make out the facial features, I felt it was a woman.

"Real fear clutched at my chest. I grabbed Nancy's arm and said, 'Look in the mirror.' But the apparition disappeared as soon as I spoke."

It is a wonderful story. But Nancy, it seems, was unsympathetic when her other half told her what he had seen. She accused him of dreaming. But, as the letter-writer asks, could one really dream the room, the furniture, and Nancy reading, just as they really were?

HERLONG MANSION

Address:	Cholakka Boulevard, Micanopy, Florida 32667
Telephone:	(904) 466-3322
Facilities:	A very elegant bed-and-breakfast in peaceful surroundings
Price Range:	Inexpensive to moderate

INN SCARLETT'S FOOTSTEPS

Concord, Georgia

IF THERE IS a taste of *Gone With the Wind* about this beautiful antebellum mansion, it is hardly surprising. Innkeepers K. C. and Vern Bassham have converted the former Magnolia Farms into a gracious southern plantation bed-and-breakfast in the style of the famous film.

There are five bedrooms, named after characters from the movie: Scarlett, Rhett, Ashley, Melanie, and Mr. Gerald. The rooms all have private bathrooms and are intended to reflect the personalities of the people for whom they are named.

Guests can relax in the library, which contains many rare Civil War volumes. There is a museum room housing the Basshams' vast collection of *Gone With the Wind* memorabilia. A walk down the grand staircase is a favorite with all visitors—particularly if they happen to meet Scarlett and Rhett look-alikes at the bottom. And there is a gift shop in the carriage house.

A full breakfast is served and can be taken on the screened porch overlooking horses grazing in the side pasture. The mansion is open for general tours every afternoon except Monday (overnight guests can do the tour without further charge). Luncheons, afternoon teas, and evening barbecues are offered to groups by prior arrangement.

Inn Scarlett's Footsteps is located in the rolling, pine-covered hills of Pike County, just south of Atlanta. Its peaceful atmosphere is a

INN SCARLETT'S FOOTSTEPS

contrast to the big city, but Atlanta Airport, Callaway Gardens, Warm Springs, Columbus, and Gordon College are all within an hour's drive.

THE GHOST at Inn Scarlett's Footsteps, according to one perhaps slightly over-imaginative guest at this *Gone With the Wind*-style bed-and-breakfast, is Rhett Butler. Clark Gable, who played the entirely fictional character in the film, might have been a bit more believable. But the elderly lady insists that Rhett appeared to her while she was attending a slumber party in the room that bears his name. By way of detail, she insists that Rhett, who obviously just didn't give a damn about the inn's no-smoking policy, was wielding a large cigar. She also claims that Rhett kissed her on the cheek.

When a bed-and-breakfast adopts such a period film theme, and does it wholeheartedly, it is hardly surprising if people get carried away by it all.

Innkeeper K. C. Bassham and her husband, Vern, have plenty of strange stories to tell. They include one extraordinary coincidence connecting the painting of the mansion in the library with the purchase of Inn Scarlett's Footsteps. Many more coincidences seem to link K. C. Bassham's style and taste with that of Miss Margaret Burkhardt, who married the owner's son and became mistress of the house in the early part of this century.

"When I came to view the estate in September 1992, I knew immediately that I was home," K. C. Basham says. "I have now learned that I act very similar to Miss Margaret, and the furniture in the main parlor is identical to the way Miss Margaret placed her furnishings, including the Governor Winthrop desk."

Perhaps Margaret Mitchell will move in next. If this story gets much better, they might even make a film about it. As Scarlett herself was fond of saying, "I'll think of it all tomorrow."

INN SCARLETT'S FOOTSTEPS

Address:	138 Hill Street, P.O. Box 138, Concord, Georgia 30206
Telephone:	(706) 495-9012, or for reservations (800) 886-7355
Facilities:	Collection of film memorabilia, guided tours
Price Range:	Inexpensive

JEKYLL ISLAND CLUB HOTEL

Jekyll Island, Georgia

A PLAYGROUND on one of the Golden Isles off the coast of Georgia, Jekyll Island is a historic monument in its own right.

Constructed in 1886, the resort has grown continuously since its inception as a retreat for a select consortium of the nation's top businessmen, including such names as Astor, Rockefeller, Morgan, Vanderbilt, and Pulitzer. From its original clubhouse there sprang a village of apartment blocks and summer cottages. Alongside these "cottages"—

in reality vast and luxurious mansions—are golf courses, marinas, and sports facilities of all kinds.

Today the Jekyll Island Club retains the grand tradition begun in the closing years of the last century. It radiates an atmosphere of luxury, exclusivity, and excellent service, although today's visitors don't need the bank balance of a Rockefeller to be able to enjoy it all.

The public rooms and guest accommodations are of a Victorian elegance and offer every modern comfort. The gourmet Grand Dining Room specializes in seafood; the deli-style Cafe Solterra will pack guests a picnic basket; and JP's Pub offers nightly entertainment. In the club's precincts, the Surfside Beach Club and the poolside bar serve snack-style meals.

Surprisingly, the club's grounds also house its own historic district, with daily guided tours investigating the original consortium's homes and the first owner's house, the 1824 DuBignon Cottage. Guests can visit the Rockefellers' cottage and other buildings including a museum and the 1904 chapel with its tiffany glass—all fully furnished with original and period items.

The one-by-nine-mile island is linked by causeway to the mainland. Jacksonville and Savannah are both an easy excursion. The Okefenokee Swamp, with its rare and abundant wildlife, is practically on the doorstep.

THE GHOST at the Jekyll Island Club Hotel is Samuel Spencer, a guest at the club in the early 1900s.

Spencer, president of the Southern Railroad Company, decided to join his fellow tycoons on vacation at the new and luxurious club on Jekyll Island. Enjoying the pampering that was—and still is—a hallmark of this extremely homey resort, Spencer developed his own routine for what became his annual stay.

He insisted on being accommodated in the "choice" apartment in the Clubhouse, an apartment with a vast marble fireplace, massive mahogany furniture, and a wide veranda offering open sea views. He also demanded that the *Wall Street Journal*, ironed smooth and folded just so, be delivered with his morning coffee. Only then could the railroad magnate settle in to enjoy his vacation amid the sea breezes of Jekyll Island.

This morning ritual continued happily for several years. Then one day in 1906, Spencer was killed in a crash between two of his own trains.

Ever since, guests occupying Spencer's preferred apartment have noticed several strange things that occur regularly each morning.

First, they find their morning paper folded differently, or opened at the business pages. Second, they find their morning coffee poured, or a full cup "sipped on," when no one else is nearby.

It seems that Samuel Spencer enjoyed his vacations here so much he still comes back. Staff reservationists are happy to point out Spencer's "choice" apartment to guests. Not everyone cares to have unseen hands helping themselves to coffee, even if it is in such an elegant and airy apartment as the one Samuel Spencer is reserving in perpetuity.

JEKYLL ISLAND CLUB HOTEL

Address:	371 Riverview Drive, Jekyll Island, Georgia 31527
Telephone:	(912) 635-2600 or (800) 333-3333
Facilities:	Fishing and water sports, "Historic District," airfield
Range:	Expensive

RITZ-CARLTON KAPALUA

Kapalua, Maui, Hawaii

MOST PEOPLE AGREE that Maui is the most beautiful of the Hawaiian islands, and the Ritz-Carlton Kapalua, a part of the superb Kapalua resort, is one of the most attractive hotels there. It would be hard to find somewhere better to stay.

To one side of the hotel, the rugged peaks of the west Maui mountain range soar toward the sky. On the other side, the sparkling Pacific Ocean stretches towards the horizon. These, or the luxuriant gardens, form the view from all 492 guest rooms and fifty-eight suites. All the rooms come complete with every modern hotel convenience, ranging from round-the-clock room service to white marble bathrooms with plush terry bath robes. Slide open the shuttered doors of your room, and there is nothing to separate you from the gentle breezes of the white sand beach.

There is a wonderful choice of places to eat. The grill serves contemporary American fare in an elegant setting. There is Hawaiian music and hula dancing in the casual Terrace Restaurant overlooking the pool. Lunch in the Banyan Tree evokes the graceful plantation era. And there's light fare available in the Beach House.

Sports facilities in the mild, year-round climate are superb. Golf on one or all of Kapalua's three famous courses, tennis (including floodlit courts), swimming, surfing, and snorkeling are popular. There's a fitness center in the hotel and a special kids' program.

Top sightseeing choices include hiking up the Haleakala Crater, helicopter trips, or whale-watching excursions from the nearby port of

Lahaina, a historic town that offers good shopping and an unexpectedly lively nightlife.

THE GHOST at the Ritz-Carlton Kapalua hasn't been seen yet—but the potential is there.

When excavation work prior to building the hotel began in December 1988, the planners' worst nightmare came true. Building workers discovered the hotel was being erected right on top of an ancient Hawaiian burial ground, containing the graves of more than one thousand native Hawaiians.

After extensive negotiations between the developers, state officials, and native Hawaiian groups, the hotel was moved to another site, and the burial ground is now being preserved as an historic park.

According to some reports, this was not the first time such a thing has happened in the Hawaiian Islands. Another major hotel hit a similar problem but continued the building work. Now mysterious shadowy figures are seen in the corridors by some guests and staff at the (not surprisingly) anonymous hotel. Hopefully, the Ritz-Carlton Kapalua has done enough to escape similar visitations, and there are no stories of anything unusual so far. But stay tuned.

RITZ-CARLTON KAPALUA

Address:	One Ritz-Carlton Drive, Kapalua, Maui, Hawaii 96761
Telephone:	(808) 669-6200
Fax:	(808) 665-0026
Facilities:	Part of a major beach resort, all major sports facilities
Price Range:	Expensive

IDAHO

THE JAMESON

Wallace, Idaho

THE HISTORIC Jameson Restaurant, Saloon, and Hotel retains a touch of the Old West in Wallace, rich in the heritage of the Coeur d'Alene mining district.

Originally opened in 1900, The Jameson was a traditional saloon and small-town hotel, now restored to its former elegance. While many similar properties have been torn down for redevelopment, The Jameson has made a feature of its old-fashioned appearance and informal atmosphere, so it still has the charm of a turn-of-the-century hotel.

The bedrooms, on the third floor, are very Victorian in appearance, with heavy wooden furniture, chunky hand-carved wooden headboards, and thick white bedspreads. The decorations and carpets are in Victorian patterns, and the rooms contain period knickknacks and pictures.

The restaurant, open daily for breakfast, lunch, and dinner, has been beautifully restored, again in the style of the early 1900s. It has a casual atmosphere, perfect for enjoying the varied menu of fine food. But the hotel's real pride and joy has to be the saloon, with its mirrored back bar, ceiling fans, and polished brass. It is the perfect spot to relive the old days, and a popular place with the locals.

The natives are definitely friendly! Coupled with the relaxing environment, this makes Wallace a pleasant and perhaps unusual destination for a short break. Local attractions include the Coeur d'Alene District Mining Museum, the Northern Pacific Depot, the Murray Goldfields, and the Cataldo Mission. The Wallace and Kellogg golf courses are both within easy reach, and in winter there is skiing on the Silverhorn and in Lookout Pass.

THE GHOST at The Jameson is Maggie, who stayed at the hotel as a long-term guest in the early part of the century. Nobody really knew where she came from, but she was in her late twenties, well dressed, obviously well-bred, and wealthy.

She would stay at the hotel—usually in her favorite Room 3—for weeks at a time, doing little except watch the activity in the streets outside the window of her twin-bedded room, relaxing in the hotel's sitting room, and sometimes helping the staff in the saloon and the steak house. Occasionally, Maggie received letters from places such as New York and London, but apart from guessing she might be of Celtic origin, hotel staff and locals alike knew nothing else about her.

This went on for years. Finally, one day early in the 1930s, Maggie checked out of the hotel for the last time. She was headed for the East Coast. A few weeks later word came back to Wallace that she had either been murdered in a train robbery or died violently in an accident. The staff at The Jameson, who had enjoyed her company and appreciated her help, were quite sad.

Several months later, according to general manager Rick Shaffer, "Odd things started to happen at The Jameson, especially on the third floor in Room 3." Room fans and lights were turned on and off by an invisible hand. Hot showers turned cold. On several occasions, guests found themselves locked in their rooms with the key on the outside and had to summon help from the street.

Says Shaffer, "Quiet footsteps, and the uneasy presence of someone who seems to be nearby but cannot be seen, were reported by guests and employees alike."

Strangest of all, someone was using the sheets and towels in Room 3 despite the fact it was locked and empty. The hotel owners, the Jamesons (who have since given it their name), were so puzzled they consulted a couple of passing psychics. After due deliberation, the psychics agreed there was a spirit at the hotel: a woman who had died violently and who, because she had no home of her own and loved the hotel, had "checked back in."

No prizes for guessing that was Maggie. She is friendly, stressed the psychics. In an odd way the Jamesons and their staff are glad to have her back.

"They felt the same comfort from her presence as they had when she was staying with them before," Shaffer says.

"To this day, Maggie makes her presence known. She is almost always welcome, and even looked forward to," Shaffer adds.

She still turns off the hot water, steals keys, and fiddles with the fans. And sometimes, judging by the sounds guests report, she even finds time for the odd spooky social gathering. Lonely Maggie, it seems, is among friends at last.

THE JAMESON

Address:	304 6th Street, Wallace, Idaho 83873
Telephone:	(208) 556-1554
Facilities:	Traditional-style saloon, turn-of-the-century atmosphere
Price Range:	Inexpensive

GRATZ PARK INN

Lexington, Kentucky

THIS BEST WESTERN hotel is a forty-four-bedroom property which, perhaps surprisingly for a hotel in this modern group, dates back to 1916. But when it was constructed, it was not planned as an hotel—it was a hospital.

Inspired by the Mayo Clinic, three local doctors joined forces to erect the colonial revival-style building which was to be the Lexington Clinic. It remained a hospital until 1958, when the clinic was moved into a new building. During its forty years of medical care, the old hospital had dealt with many strange cases, including one hardy patient who had a stick stuck in his eye for fifteen years, the painful result of trying to escape the tax men after he was caught distilling moonshine whiskey.

The old hospital became an engineering works for a while, then stood empty until it was converted into the new Gratz Park Inn in 1987. The conversion has been an excellent one. The hotel's thirty-eight regular guest rooms, four junior suites, and two luxury suites all have nineteenth-century antique reproduction furniture and mahogany four-poster beds. All have private facilities, telephones, and TV.

Room rates include complimentary continental breakfast. Other perks range from a free daily newspaper and free local telephone calls to a complimentary limo service to and from Blue Grass Airport. Free coffee is served in the lobby round-the-clock, and business services include on-site fax and photocopying. Columbia's Restaurant serves all main meals and operates room service.

The hotel is in the heart of Lexington's historical district and only three blocks from the business district. Shopping in Victorian Square is nearby. Local attractions such as the Keeneland Race Course, Red Mile Harness Track, Kentucky Horse Park, and the world-famous Bluegrass Thoroughbred horse farms are only a short drive from Gratz Park Inn.

THE GHOSTS at the Gratz Park Inn are presumably inherited from the building's days as a hospital. They appeared immediately after the reopening in 1987. Diana Stevie, the hotel's director of sales and marketing, takes up the story:

"Soon after we opened, a customer came up to the guest services desk, upset because there was a little girl on the second floor playing with her jacks in front of the elevator. When he called out to her, she laughed and ran around the corner. The guest followed her, to make sure she got to her room safely, but when he turned the corner the little girl had vanished into thin air."

Hotel staff promptly christened the little girl "Anna." She makes frequent appearances in front of both staff and visitors.

"Guests often comment on the cute little girl upstairs dressed in Victorian clothing and ask if she is going to be in some sort of competition or play," Diana Stevie says.

Anna laughs, sings, and plays with her dolls as well as her jacks. Often, she tries to play hide-and-seek with hotel employees.

"We will see her open a closet door and hide, but when we open the door, she has disappeared," Stevie says. "Then you'll hear her laughter ringing down the hall and see her skirt as she turns the corner. But, needless to say, when we chase after her, she's nowhere to be found."

Stevie and other hotel employees reckon the more they play with Anna, the more the sightings increase.

"She is our most frequently seen resident," Stevie laughs.

Not quite so amusing is "John," a mischievous spirit who likes to awaken guests in the middle of the night by turning on the radio or TV sets at full volume.

"Sometimes you can even hear his laughter reverberating down the hallway after you," Stevie says. "John gives our guests quite a scare sometimes, but we know he is just having a good time."

There are more good times going on that visitors don't always appreciate. Guests on the third floor sometimes ring down to the front desk to complain of people pacing around in the room above theirs, or a loud party in progress. Staff have to gently point out to such complainants that there isn't a room above theirs. The third floor is the hotel's top floor.

One other phantom at the Gratz Park Inn is a strange black man who sometimes wanders into the laundry room and just stands there without speaking, looking forlorn. He can give the housekeepers a nasty turn, especially when he disappears. Who is he, and what is he doing? The hotel has one clue. "Back in the early 1900s, our laundry room was the county morgue," says Diana Stevie.

No wonder there's free coffee in the lobby, round-the-clock.

GRATZ PARK INN

Address:	120 West Second Street, Lexington, Kentucky 40507
Telephone:	(606) 231-1777 or (800) 227-4362
Fax:	(606) 233-7593
Facilities:	Extensive Best Western standard guest and business facilities
Price Range:	Moderate

LOUISIANA

DELTA QUEEN

New Orleans, Louisiana

THE *DELTA QUEEN* is one of a trio of traditional overnight stern-wheel paddle steamers that run year-round, offering three- to twelve-night cruises on the Mississippi, Cumberland, and Ohio Rivers from New Orleans, going as far north as Minneapolis/St. Paul and Pittsburgh. Unlike her modern sister ships, the *Delta Queen*—launched in 1927—doesn't just look authentic, she *is* authentic. As such, she has been officially designated as a national historic landmark since 1989.

A holiday on the 3,360-ton wedding-cake style *Delta Queen* has more than a touch of history about it, too. With a top speed of twelve miles per hour, her progress up the rivers of the great American heartland can be stately, but the surroundings are sumptuous: from teakwood handrails to gleaming brass fittings and Tiffany-style stained-glass windows.

The centerpiece of the ship is the elegant grand staircase, lit by crystal chandeliers. Public rooms are spacious. There's an excellent restaurant (the Orleans Dining Room), several lounges and a cozy bar, and the food and entertainment seem to be nonstop.

Accommodations match this grand style: many of the suites and staterooms have brass beds and they all have a river view. But standards have been improved a bit since the ship was built, and each of the ninety-one cabins (the Delta Queen Steamboat Company prefers to call them "rooms") is now climate controlled and has a private bath and plush wall-to-wall carpeting. A crew of seventy-five looks after passengers' every need.

DELTA QUEEN

You half expect to meet bearded trappers, silver-tongued card-sharps, and beautiful crinoline-clad southern belles on a cruise like this, and you might not be disappointed. Locals don traditional dress to go down to the levee and meet the *Delta Queen* when she makes her daily stops at a riverside city or town. How do they know she's coming? The steam calliope on deck, pounding out tunes like "I'm Forever Blowing Bubbles" during twice-daily concerts, can be heard from miles away and still evokes from river folk the cry Mark Twain would recognize, "Steamboat's a-comin'."

THE GHOST on board the *Delta Queen* is Captain Mary Greene of the steamship-owning Greene family. In the 1940s, she was one of only two qualified female pilots on the Mississippi. A formidable woman, whose picture still hangs in the ship's Betty Blake Lounge, she was the pilot of the *Delta Queen* when the ship was first moved from San Francisco to the Mississippi in 1947. Because she was a strict teetotaler, she did not allow any bars on board—and that remained the rule until 1949, when Captain Greene died aboard the ship in what is now Cabin 109.

After Mary Greene's death, the owners of the *Delta Queen* quickly responded to passenger demand to open the ship's first bar in the forward passenger lounge. But the matriarchal figure who had ruled the ship with an iron rod still seemed to be around, and expecting her instructions to be carried out. A series of unexplained accidents in the bar reached a bizarre climax when the *Delta Queen* was rammed by one of the giant barges that ply the Mississippi and are often named after famous river folk. As the barge crunched through the forward passenger lounge windows, the crew of the *Delta Queen* gazed in utter disbelief at the name on the prow. It was *Mary Greene*.

Engineers eventually separated the two ships, but nobody could separate the *Delta Queen* from its river-going specter. The present skipper, Captain Gabriel Chengary, is among many members of the crew, as well as passengers, who have seen Captain Mary Greene.

Chengary's story is quite fascinating. Dressed in a green housecoat, rather than any sort of nautical uniform, Mary Greene is frequently spotted in and around the bars and lounges, Chengary says. She has also been seen in Cabin 106. She seems to have overcome her antipathy to alcohol, for transoms in the forward passenger lounge open and close of their own accord, as Captain Greene ensures that everything is shipshape. She has even turned up at the present captain's cocktail party, opening the door and closing it behind her.

One of her most startling appearances was in the Betty Blake Lounge, when a woman passenger sleeping in one of the cabins opening off the lounge came out of her room during the night to get a book. She saw an apparently quite solid, green-housecoated figure in the otherwise empty lounge and, making polite conversation one might expect between fellow passengers in the small hours, explained that she couldn't sleep. The woman in the green housecoat smiled and nodded sympathetically but did not speak. Only later did the insomniac passenger realize she hadn't previously seen the woman in the green housecoat. She told her story to Captain Chengary and he took her into the wheelhouse and showed her a picture of Captain Mary Greene.

"That's her," exclaimed the passenger. "Who is she?"

Not everyone enjoys such stories, however, and as Captain Chengary was telling it, two of our fellow passengers—both of them elderly women—protested. The captain had no right to frighten people with such tales, they said. As charming as ever, despite being interrupted during a private conversation, Captain Chengary replied politely, "I am captain of this ship, and I have every right to give this gentleman factual accounts of things I have witnessed."

Two fellow passengers also had personal experiences with Mary Greene. Sherry Vetter, a garage owner's wife from Oakland, California, told how on a previous cruising holiday on the *Delta Queen* with her mother-in-law, also named Mary, she had come down with a touch of flu. Sweating and feverish, she spent the day in their cabin off the Betty Blake Lounge. Later, she thanked her mother-in-law for coming into the cabin during the day, silently soothing her brow, and offering her aspirin.

"But Sherry," Mary replied, "I didn't come near you all day. I've been on a shore excursion."

Sherry protested that none of the other passengers knew she was ill. But she hadn't dreamt it. Somebody had come into her cabin, offered her aspirin, and soothed her brow. She remembered her distinctly: a mature woman, wearing a green housecoat.

DELTA QUEEN

Address:	Delta Queen Steamboat Co., Robin Street Wharf, New Orleans, Louisiana 70130-1890
Telephone:	Inquiries (504) 586-0631 or (800) 543-7637. Reservations (800) 543-1949 or through travel agent
Fax:	(504) 585-0630
Facilities:	Private baths in every cabin, full meal service, lounges and bar, on-board entertainments, air conditioning, boat-to-riverbank telephones
Price Range:	Expensive

DUFOUR-BALDWIN HOUSE

New Orleans, Louisiana

THE DUFOUR-BALDWIN HOUSE, on historic Esplanade Avenue, is one of the most important antebellum residences in New Orleans. It is also the only plantation-size bed-and-breakfast in the metropolitan area, and it reflects the romance of life during the golden age of New Orleans.

The house was built in 1859 for Cyprien Dufour, a prominent New Orleans attorney and state senator. Designed by the architect Henry Howard, it is a classic example of the Italianate-late Greek revival style and presents a magnificently pillared frontage to Esplanade Avenue.

A beautiful home during the nineteenth century, it spent much of the twentieth century as an apartment building, and during that time the fabric deteriorated badly. Finally, the house was left empty for three years, a prey to vandals and the elements.

But in 1989, it was purchased by attorney Elizabeth Williams and her partner, Rick Normand. They began the tedious, expensive task of renovating the house and gardens. The work was scheduled for completion by fall 1995. The house is to have nine guest rooms, with the gardens fully landscaped and fenced. Then the entire property will once again be one of the most beautiful in a city home to numerous architectural wonders.

The house is full of antiques, many of them original to the property. Likewise, the bedrooms are charming. Breakfast is served privately or in the garden. Children are welcome; smokers are not. Because of the historic nature of the house, smoking is permitted only outside.

The French Quarter is within walking distance of the house, and the city's convention center and business district are only five minutes away by cab. Personalized information is available about restaurants, arts and cultural events, museums, sightseeing, and shopping (especially for antiques).

THE GHOST at the Dufour-Baldwin House is Arthemise Bouligny, the wife of the original owner of the house, Albert Baldwin, who died in 1911. Blissfully happy in the house during her lifetime (and in the property's heyday), Arthemise Bouligny appears to have stayed on after her death. She is often seen in and around one of the front guest bedrooms—on the left-hand side of the house as you face it, over the side door—which used to be her room.

Arthemise's room, formerly known as the Red Room, has since been renamed the Henry Howard Room. As the story goes, Arthemise liked to appear on the balcony, particularly in the early morning. Upon inspection, the room certainly seemed to have a slightly strange atmosphere, even though it was very warm and welcoming.

The french windows overlooking the balcony were heavily curtained, and when I awoke in the morning I hardly dared to look through them in case I saw Arthemise. The curtains were stirring and there was a shadow beyond them. I expect it was the shadow cast by the dressing-table's tall mirror, except when I looked again, it had gone.

Ennis Brown is the new manager of the bed-and-breakfast side of the business. One day while working in the narrow hallway connecting the Henry Howard Room with its private bathroom, Brown glanced into the room and saw Arthemise Bouligny standing there, looking at him. As he walked toward her, she vanished.

Construction worker Robert Marksberry has had an even closer encounter with her. During the renovation, he was standing on a stepladder in the Henry Howard Room changing a light bulb, when the curtains stirred and Arthemise, dressed in a long turn-of-the-century gown, stepped through the french windows and into the room. Helpless on top of his ladder, Marksberry ("I nearly fell off from shock") could do nothing but gaze in fascination as Arthemise walked toward him. Then she slowly faded away into nothingness.

It is all very galling for Williams, Normand, and their children. They are longing to meet the ghost but have never seen her.

"She seems to be avoiding us," Liz says. "I expect she is waiting until she can catch us on the top of a ladder."

DUFOUR-BALDWIN HOUSE

Address:	1707 Esplanade Avenue, New Orleans, Louisiana 70116
Telephone:	(504) 945-1503
Facilities:	Residents' lounge, antique furnishings
Price Range:	Inexpensive

LLOYD HALL PLANTATION

Cheneyville, Louisiana

LLOYD HALL is a plantation home right out of the gentle days preceding "the late unpleasantness." An antebellum home on the banks of Bayou Boeuf, Lloyd Hall had so fallen into decay, it had disappeared in the undergrowth sometime after the depression. But it reappeared almost magically when the parents of its present owner bought the land in the 1940s.

Now beautifully restored, Lloyd Hall is in the care of Dr. and Mrs. Frank Fitzgerald. As well as being a working 640-acre plantation of cotton, corn, and a few friendly cattle, it is their home and offers at-home accommodations for a small number of guests.

One guest suite is in a separate cottage, with its own kitchen, open fireplace, and two bedrooms. The remaining accommodations are in the Old Kitchen: two suites, again with open fireplaces. Each suite is furnished in a comfortable, rustic style.

That makes the big house all the more breathtaking. It has ornate plasterwork ceilings, a sweeping suspended staircase, tall-pillared portico, and wonderfully fragrant rose gardens. But its great treasures are in the rooms, filled with elegant furniture from the 1800s, gleaming in the light of the great crystal chandeliers. Paintings, embroideries, and objets d'art all add to the atmosphere, as do the sit-down dinners served on the long mahogany dining table.

Lloyd Hall is a three-hour drive from the cosmopolitan delights of New Orleans and a mere one and a half hours from the colorful river town of Natchez, Mississippi. Lafayette, an hour to the south, is the "capital" of Cajun country, with its folk museum, the Acadian Village, and town museum honoring the great regional carnivals of Mardi Gras.

THE GHOST at the Lloyd Hall Plantation is Harry, a young dark-haired Union soldier.

Harry deserted his regiment during the Civil War for the love of a young girl of the Lloyd family. He used to visit her secretly in the dead of the night. One night, just as Harry was preparing to serenade his sweetheart with love songs on the violin, the men of the family set upon him. They intended to beat some sense into him and return him to his regiment to face possible court-martial. But in the scuffle Harry was killed.

Harry, it seems, cannot bear to be parted from his love, or from Lloyd Hall. He returns regularly and has been seen by many guests and staff on the upstairs balcony where he used to meet his sweetheart. Just as midnight strikes, the figure of a young dark-haired soldier dressed in blue seems to float up from beneath the house, from the very spot where Harry was buried hastily in a shallow grave. He comes to rest on the balcony, preparing to play his violin and serenade his love.

Harry is probably Lloyd Hall's most visible ghost. But he is not its only intangible resident and possibly not its most important. That title must go to an early owner, William Lloyd, who seems to have attracted trouble wherever he went during his lifetime.

Visitors to the plantation today can see Indian arrows embedded in the dining room door, relics of a Choctaw raid during William Lloyd's tenure, before the Civil War.

During the war itself, Lloyd had an eye on the best chance of personal survival, as well as that of his plantation. He managed to keep peace with both the Union and the Confederacy by trading secrets. But one day, his luck as a double agent ran out. On his way north to the battle of Mansfield, carrying vital information to the Confederates about the strength of Union forces in the area, he was caught by a Yankee scouting party. Lloyd was hastily tried as a traitor and hanged from a tree on his own plantation.

He still watches over his property, strolling its corridors, a tall figure in a dark suit, with red hair and a bushy beard.

William Lloyd's niece, Inez, is also an intangible resident. She committed suicide because of a broken heart not long after the Civil War. And the family's mammy, Amy, can't seem to bring herself to leave her charges. She is often spotted rocking beside the fire in the back parlor, a room not normally open to visitors.

These four are the only ghosts at the plantation recognizable in form, appearing as misty outlines.

But there must be many more spirits lodged within this stout brick home to account for all the strange happenings reported over the years by family members, staff, and plantation workers alike.

Formal dinners regularly take place amid great pomp in the great dining room. Despite frequent checks by housekeepers, there is always at least one item missing from the table as dinner is served—it could be a glass, a salt shaker, even a napkin.

The ghosts love their food, too. Cooking smells waft through the house at odd hours—even at 4:00 A.M.—when the kitchens are dark and silent. Sometimes the ovens or the lights switch on and off for no reason. Doors open and close and the doorbell rings.

The ghosts play other tricks, too. Once, when a tour group was being shown around the house, a crystal bowl shot off the piano, flew across the room, and shattered on the rug.

All these accounts are confirmed by staff member Beulah Davis. Psychics have investigated the house and their findings revealed hints of great animosity among the spirits and the departed members of the Lloyd family. But no one has ever found this phantom family feud or the spirits in the least bit frightening.

But for the best guide to Lloyd Hall's ghostly goings-on, watch the cats.

According to Davis, they are unusually laid back and quiet. "But sometimes they just ball up in a knot, with their hair standing up on their backs and their eyes turning around in their heads. If you can't see spirits, you won't see what the cats are seeing. But if the house pops or cracks real loud, then it's a ghost coming in or going out."

Davis adds, "I feel real safe with the ghosts. I know they won't harm me."

LLOYD HALL PLANTATION

Address:	292 Lloyd Bridge Road, Cheneyville, Louisiana 71325
Telephone:	(318) 776-5641
Fax:	(318) 279-2335
Facilities:	Working cotton plantation
Price Range:	Moderate

MYRTLES PLANTATION

St. Francisville, Louisiana

ONE OF THE oldest plantation houses in the Deep South, the Myrtles is a long arcaded building serene behind its shutters and its decorative wrought-iron work.

St. Francisville, on the Mississippi, is often spoken of as being "in English Louisiana." And indeed, this pretty settlement does seem frozen in time, with an air of having scarcely progressed beyond the turn of the century.

By then, of course, the Myrtles was already "old family." The plantation itself was founded in the late eighteenth century by General David Bradford. The building, many of its beautiful contents, and its grove of 150 majestic live oaks have survived the rigors of the Civil War, the ravages of the depression, and the invasion of "new money."

Today it is in the safe hands of John and Teeta Moss, who offer guests the gracious living of yesteryear among the grand furnishings of this very stately mansion. The nine guest rooms are richly furnished with mantels of marble from Carrara; ornate ormolu cabinets and mirrors; and furniture heavy in gold leaf or *faux-bois*. Walls and ceilings boast ornate plasterwork and are hung with aubusson tapestries. Guests dine under Baccarat chandeliers and take their coffee and after-dinner drinks on the Long Gallery, framed in lacy ironwork typical of the Spanish influences of the area and at its best in nearby New Orleans. But for all its grandeur, the Myrtles is a "stately home" where guests immediately feel at home.

St. Francisville stands beside Ol' Man River. And only a short drive—or cruise—away are the big-city attractions of Baton Rouge and New Orleans.

THE GHOST at the Myrtles Plantation is more a gaggle of ghouls—none of which is in the least bit frightening.

At last count, there were fourteen of them. The Myrtles makes a good claim to the title of "America's Most Haunted House."

MYRTLES PLANTATION

Most of the extraordinary happenings at the Myrtles are well documented and have recurred frequently during the house's two-hundred-year history. Its very location must predispose the building to be haunted. It's built on ground sacred to Native Americans—a Tunica burial site.

Frances Kermeen, owner since around 1980, had just moved in when she heard voices calling softly and insistently for "Sarah." Alone in the house, Kermeen checked all the rooms, but there was no trace of anyone. Later she discovered that two Sarahs had lived in the house in the early 1800s.

Might these Sarahs be the two blonde girls in white dresses who are sometimes glimpsed floating down the plantation house's long hallways? Or are the faint figures those of the two daughters of Judge Clarke Woodruffe, son-in-law to General Bradford, who were poisoned by the Myrtles's most famous ghost, Chloe?

Chloe was the girls' mammy. And she had an insatiable curiosity. She just *had* to know what the family was talking about behind closed doors. One day the judge caught her listening in to a somewhat shady business deal. A hot-tempered man, he meted out a macabre, immediate punishment. He sliced off Chloe's ear.

Chloe planned a dreadful revenge. On the little girls' birthday she baked a cake, decorating it prettily with a lethal frosting. The children died in agony.

This time Chloe's punishment came from her fellow slaves. She was seized and summarily hanged from one of the great live oaks beside the house. Her body was then flung into the Mississippi.

But Chloe still listens at doors in the Myrtles. Kermeen has heard and seen her: a young woman wearing a green kerchief pulled low on one side of her head. Chloe even bent over her bed one night—just as she did to a pair of honeymooners staying in the house in the early 1980s. The bride was so alarmed that the couple checked out then and there.

Perhaps it is Chloe tidying up who resets the heating thermostats and switches lights off and on. Or are these pranks the work of one of the other ghosts in the house, who all seem to go through their paces several times a week?

There are often the noises of children laughing at play, and of others crying pitifully, when none are in the house.

Guests staying in the house during May and June might encounter a young, badly wounded Confederate soldier in one of the bedrooms. He seems to be having a leg wound dressed by unseen hands.

Three Union soldiers are also in residence. It is known that they were shot in a skirmish on the property.

Then there is a "grump" (says Kermeen) who occasionally hurls a clock or a candlestick across the drawing room.

The "youngest" ghost seems to be that of an overseer, stabbed in a robbery at the house in 1927.

There is also a slender young man in a fancy vest who was stabbed in the house over a gambling debt.

A dramatic scenario is reenacted regularly, too, when the figure of a frock-coated man is seen to stagger backward from the front door as if shot, and reel up the stairs before collapsing on the seventeenth stair to die. Look closely as you go up, and you can see a dark discoloration in the polished wood, an ancient bloodstain that no amount of work can remove.

But the last remaining recorded "ghost" is actually a jolly and lively happening. When everyone in the house is tucked into bed, and the building is shuttered and silent for the night, there is a sudden burst of music, laughter, and the clink of glasses. There is a ball in progress at the big house.

MYRTLES PLANTATION

Address: Highway 61, Box 1100, St. Francisville, Louisiana 70775
Telephone: (504) 635-6277
Fax: (504) 635-5837
Facilities: Plantation-style bed-and-breakfast, antiques, gardens
Price Range: Moderate

OAK ALLEY

Vacherie, Louisiana

OAK ALLEY is an antebellum plantation home in the grand manner. Its Greek revival-style facade is protected from the mighty Mississippi by a levee with a private landing stage, from which an avenue of massive live oaks stretches a full quarter-mile up to the front porch.

Not that the house was originally named Oak Alley. When it was built by Jacques Roman in the 1830s, he chose a spot at the end of a row of tiny trees planted by a former landowner, and Roman's wife, Celine, named her new home *Beau Sejour*. Those little trees became the great, intertwined live oaks of today—such a landmark that contemporary riverboat captains took to calling the Romans' landing Oak Alley.

The house fell into disrepair in the early years of this century. Now restored, it is filled with authentic wallpapers, gleaming furniture with an almost feminine delicacy about it, and soft, lacy drapes. It is a style attributed to Celine Roman, whose taste created the lovely soft-pink mansion and its deep veranda and soaring colonnade.

Guest accommodations are in five rooms, some in the main house itself, others in beautifully restored Creole cottages just beside the big house. All are fitted to a high degree of modern comfort, but with many atmospheric and antique touches—magazines from the 1920s to browse through, photographs from the family albums of the Romans and their successors, including the Stewarts (last private owners of the plantation), and all the little objets d'art that make this grand house a home.

Oak Alley is set among rural scenery. Local attractions include hunting, fishing, and swamp tours. But the French colonial charm and glittering sophistication of New Orleans is only a short drive away. Vacherie is a splendid base for exploring Cajun country, too. Many other beautiful plantation properties in the neighborhood are open to visitors.

THE GHOST at Oak Alley is Louise, daughter of Jacques and Celine Roman.

Louise, like any well-bred Creole girl in the years immediately preceding the Civil War, would not tolerate the slightest impropriety in matters of courting. Imagine her distress and the distress of her mother, Celine, when Louise's suitor rode up the broad avenue of live oaks in a very unsteady manner and arrived at the front door roaring drunk!

Louise fled up the steep stairs to the sanctuary of her own room. But she slipped, catching her heel in her crinoline petticoat, and fell. The wire supporting the crinoline hoop tore from its sheath and cut into Louise's leg, causing a wound that refused to heal.

Not unusual for those days, gangrene set in. To save her life, this pretty, blonde southern belle had to have her leg amputated below the knee. This meant an end to her dancing days, and an end to her hopes of marriage. Embittered, Louise chose to enter a nunnery in St. Louis. Later she founded her own convent in New Orleans, spending her last years near her family.

When she died, she was buried with her amputated leg beside her. The livid limb had been preserved for her by her loving mother in a tiny tomb in the garden at Oak Alley.

A gruesome tale, perhaps. But the story is rather in keeping with the image of Oak Alley as it has been portrayed in the many films on supernatural subjects made there over the years. Latest in the line is *Interview with the Vampire*, which shows, for a split second, the little tomb made for Louise's leg.

Louise's spirit enjoys the run of the house. She's been spotted in one of the bedrooms. Not with the naked eye, I hasten to add, but as a crinolined blonde girl seated on a chair in a photograph taken by a visitor in what he was certain was an empty room.

And she seems to resent the able-bodied. Tourist guides in the house, who regularly hurry up and down the stairs in the course of their work, often feel something pinching at their legs as they go. Later, little black-and-blue bruises show up, always below the knee.

One of the guides, Alma Mitchell, often suffers these pesky assaults. And, she says, she has often felt the presence of another person standing close beside her when she was otherwise alone.

Other guides have heard footsteps following them, or echoing on the floor above. Helen Dumas, Mitchell's colleague, has heard a number of unexplained noises, among them the sound of a horse and carriage pulling up to the front porch. Tight-lipped, she says, "I don't believe in ghosts. But you do hear some mighty peculiar things in this house."

The house's tourist guides are not alone in seeing and hearing things. The "sensitive" photographer apart, many guests and visitors have been allowed a glimpse or sound of Oak Alley's past. One psychic investigator declares the house to be "alive" with the spirits of its long-gone inhabitants. One bedroom in particular seems to be the haunt of all the babies and children of the house. It's the room where Mrs. Stewart, last private owner of the plantation, slept and where she died in 1972. Her dark-clad form is sometimes glimpsed reflected in the tall pier glass.

But perhaps the most poignant spirit of Oak Alley is that of a woman dressed in deep mourning, in a black crinoline and black flowing veil. Visitors often ask who it might be up on the widow's walk, the balustraded gallery right on the crown of the roof, where the bereaved could take the air in suitable seclusion.

The same figure has been seen galloping on horseback, veil flying, down the avenue of trees toward the levee. And sometimes the widow is also seen on the second- and third-floor balconies, areas not open to staff or to visitors.

It seems to be Celine Roman looking for her husband Jacques who died of tuberculosis in the house in 1848, just nine years after the building was completed.

Celine often paced the widow's walk, watching for the Mississippi riverboats that regularly brought her husband back from his business trips. When she saw the paddle wheeler rounding the bend, she would rush down to the levee to greet him. She seems to be searching for him still.

OAK ALLEY

  Address: 3645 LA Highway 18, Vacherie, Louisiana 70090
 Telephone: (504) 265-2151
  Facilities: Historic plantation, guest rooms, memorabilia, gardens
 Price Range: Moderate

T'FRERE'S HOUSE
Lafayette, Louisiana

T'FRERE'S HOUSE, built around 1890 by Oneziphore Comeaux, is now a luxuriously comfortable and highly atmospheric bed-and-breakfast.

With just three guest bedrooms, all with private baths, T'Frere's House offers a rather special *en famille* atmosphere. Its cypress walls and Cajun-style furnishings all reflect the care of recent owners to preserve the essence of Cajun culture and cuisine.

Breakfasts at T'Frere's House are legendary, for innkeepers Pat and Maugie Pastor pride themselves on their presentation of the dishes of the bayou country.

There's a broad veranda to rest on in the cool of the evening, enjoying one of the Pastors' special "T'Juleps" and a selection of Cajun canapés. There is a smokers' retreat on the gallery above the front door, and there are gardens full of great oaks, a charming gazebo, and camellias in which to wander.

The kitchen still has the Comeaux family fireplace, though the comfortable sitting and dining rooms have been somewhat "gentrified" over the years. Guest rooms are neat and homey with fresh chintzes and soft drapes. T'Frere's House is on the outskirts of Lafayette, "capital" of Louisiana's Cajun Country. The city itself houses the Acadian Village and a living history folk museum in the form of a typical bayou town of yesteryear. The Lafayette Museum has a special section celebrating the glamour and traditions of Mardi Gras. And there is a nature station devoted to the wildlife of the bayous.

THE GHOST at T'Frere's House is Amelie. Amelie seems to be a permanent resident at the old Comeaux house. The present innkeepers, the Pastors, do not lay any special claim to sightings of Amelie. But their predecessors, the Moseleys, knew her as an old and trusted friend.

Amelie is a tiny woman, dressed in turn-of-the-century Cajun style. Peggy Moseley reports meeting her first on a summer's afternoon when she was surprised to find all her lingerie laid out neatly on the bed upstairs. Moseley and her housekeeper, Louella, had only just finished putting it all away in a chest in the downstairs hall.

Being new to the house at that time, Moseley resolutely put any fanciful thoughts from her mind. But a couple of weeks later, when she was alone in the house and telephoning a friend, she heard some terrifying crashes and splintering noises coming from the direction of the pantry. Dropping the telephone and running to investigate, Moseley found that something—or someone—had swept all the jars of preserves and other foodstuffs off the shelves to the stone floor, where they were smashed.

Moseley began to put two and two together. "I felt the house must contain something outside the sensory world," she reported. She began to be aware of something unseen about the house, a mischievous spirit who spoke French.

Undaunted, Peggy Moseley summoned a French-speaking friend and had him tell the empty air, "In God's name, I'll burn the house down if you misbehave." And she added, "Leave my children alone, leave me alone! And if you wish to go on living here, there are house rules!"

Peace prevailed, although Amelie, as the spirit came to be called, seemed to dislike hymns played on the piano. She splattered candle wax all over the keys and the polished lid whenever hymns were played—times when there was no draft to account for the wax.

One of the Moseleys' neighbors identified Amelie as an unhappy woman who had died in the house in an accident at the age of thirty-two. Moseley's mother saw Amelie in the garden, describing her as "a little Cajun lady, wearing her hair in a bun, dressed in a gown of ashes-of-roses color, with a cleft chin. She spoke French."

"A pity," said Peggy Moseley's mother. "She was so nice. I'd have liked to talk to her."

Amelie's mischievousness took a rather naughty turn at the wedding of the Moseleys' daughter, Mary. The homemade punch, tasty and golden, suddenly turned a bilious green. On inquiry, it appeared that Amelie had been spotted in the kitchen, pouring liberal quantities of green food coloring into the punch bowl.

Amelie plays the piano and sits translucent in a rocker on the porch. She gazes down on visitors from an upstairs window and apparently causes mysterious green lights to rise through the hall floorboards.

As for Amelie being a trusted friend, that came later. Amid all this mischief, Amelie took time out to help the Moseleys' son, Matthew, with his studies, explaining a thorny problem to him during the night with the aid of a chalkboard she had with her. She also took care of Peggy Moseley, alone in bed with a dose of flu, wrapping her up in a comforter that had been downstairs on the back of a sofa.

Perhaps Amelie was trying to prevent the same fate befalling Peggy as had overtaken Amelie herself. The tiny Cajun woman drowned in the cistern at the back of the house while delirious with fever.

Amelie saved the whole family—and her former home—from devastation by fire. One night, the Moseleys awoke to find Amelie tugging at Peggy's arm and the room full of smoke. A fire had started in the dishwasher downstairs.

Says Peggy Moseley, "I am sure she is just lost. I tell her this is my time; your time is somewhere else."

But, wherever Amelie is in time, she seems very closely tied to T'Frere's House.

T'FRERE'S HOUSE

Address:	1905 Verot School Road, Lafayette, Louisiana 70508
Telephone:	(800) 984-9347
Facilities:	Antique-filled "landmark" bed-and-breakfast, gardens
Price Range:	Medium

CASTINE INN

Castine, Maine

THIS IS A wonderful summer base for exploring the wild Atlantic coastline of Maine: a bright and friendly inn, with a magnificently muraled dining room offering an equally magnificent menu.

The inn has practiced the art of hospitality since it was built in 1898. Guests arriving by car today are greeted just as warmly as those who once disembarked from boats at the town wharf (a mode of transport still chosen by some). A flower-filled front porch, someone to help with the bags, and a spot of iced tea are just the beginning of a wonderful experience that every inn should be imitating.

The maritime scenery of Penobscot Bay is justly famous, so it's fitting that many of the guest rooms offer sea views. The bedrooms, which include two suites, are furnished in the style of a cottage and have private bathrooms. Children over the age of five are welcome, and overnight rates include a full breakfast.

There is a glimpse of the sea to be found in the dining room, too, although guests might find their eyes drawn to Margaret Parker's lovely murals. The menu features plenty of seafood, including local specialties such as steamed Maine lobster. Prices are extremely reasonable. Because the inn is licensed, wines are available to go with the meal. The inn also has its own pub.

Castine, perched on a seaside hill, is one of the prettiest towns in coastal Maine, with plenty of handsome nineteenth-century houses. The town square is one of the loveliest in New England, and the dark blue waters of the harbor are dotted with sailing ships.

Penobscot Bay windjammers often tie up at the town wharf. The Wilson Museum on Perkins Street helps set the local scene, and the forty-mile drive from Castine to Stonington is a scenic delight. Especially worth visiting is the Acadia National Park on Mount Desert Island.

THE GHOST at the Castine Inn came as a bit of a surprise to the owners because the author seems to have known about it before innkeepers Mark and Margaret Hodesh.

"This inn is not haunted," came the reply to initial inquiries. But the famous veteran British travel writer Kenneth Westcott-Jones and photographer Tony Hudson hold a different view.

"The Castine Inn is definitely haunted," Westcott-Jones says. "I am sure of that. It is the only place I've ever seen a ghost."

Westcott-Jones and Hudson were guests at the Castine Inn during the British general election in 1983 and stayed up very late waiting for the first results to come through on TV. Westcott-Jones was particularly interested to learn the result of the poll in his own outer-London constituency, but as the night dragged on without any news, he eventually went to bed and quickly fell asleep.

Some time later, he awoke to see the shadowy figure of a man in his room. He recalls, "I thought it was Tony Hudson, with news of the election. I said, 'Who won Croydon North-East, Tony?' but the figure didn't reply. It just looked at me. Then I woke up properly and shouted, 'What the hell's going on?' and snapped on the bedside light. And the figure, who looked like an elderly man in waterproof clothing, just faded slowly away."

The phlegmatic Westcott-Jones went back to sleep, although he says, "I still didn't know the result in Croydon North-East." Next morning, feeling slightly bereft of both poll information and rest, Westcott-Jones questioned Tony Hudson, who assured him he had not been near the room or played any tricks. Wescott-Jones then reported the incident to a member of the inn's staff, who asked his room number (which he no longer recalls), then said unconcernedly, "Oh, that would have been the old fisherman."

If such nocturnal tales are the Hodeshes' idea of a nightmare, they have one consolation. Westcott-Jones and Hudson—who have both traveled very widely over the years—are insistent that the Castine Inn is one of the best places to stay in the entire region.

CASTINE INN

Address:	Main Street, P.O. Box 41, Castine, Maine 04421
Telephone:	(207) 326-4365
Fax:	(207) 326-4570
Facilities:	Excellent dining
Price Range:	Inexpensive to moderate

KENNEBUNK INN

Kennebunk, Maine

THE KENNEBUNK INN, built in 1799, has been welcoming travelers to historic Kennebunk Village since 1920, and the same standards of hospitality and service are offered to this day.

Open all year, this classic New England inn features thirty-four charming guest rooms. All are furnished with antiques and period furniture, and most with private bath. The parlor is a favorite public room for guests to relax by the fire with a book from the inn's own library.

Room prices include a continental breakfast. However, lunch and dinner are also served by the inn, which has a proud reputation for its award-winning regional cuisine. Sunday brunch is a special feature, as is meeting old and new friends over a drink in the cozy pub. There is ample free parking on the premises.

The inn's flexible facilities enable it to host small corporate meetings and social events. Outdoor receptions in the private courtyard are accommodated.

Conveniently located in downtown Kennebunk, just ninety minutes from Boston, the inn is only minutes from the ocean. Exploring Maine's famous seashore, mountains, and lakes is a favorite pastime for visitors. But there are museums, tennis, and golf nearby, and the inn is an ideal base for a spot of bargain-hunting. Antique shops abound in Kennebunk itself, while the factory outlet shops in Freeport and Kittery are only a short drive away.

THE GHOST at the Kennebunk Inn is believed to be Silas Perkins, a night watchman and auditor at the inn who was working there in the 1960s when he died of a heart attack. Silas was a well-known local character, who came from a seafaring family and wrote excellent poetry in his spare time. When he died in his eighties, he was much mourned.

By all accounts he is still around, although some locals say it is an older ghost. A presence has been felt in the Kennebunk Inn's cellar. Someone plays pranks in the bar by occasionally causing mugs or glasses to levitate, and mischief has also been reported in Room 8. Staff readily admit that the inn is haunted. When Alex and Kathy Pratt bought the property in 1991, they found a legal disclaimer in the purchase-and-sales agreement notifying the buyers of a resident ghost named Silas. Silas is known to be friendly, but to the disappointment of staff and guests alike, he hasn't been seen lately.

The stories about Silas began when the former owners, Arthur and Angela LeBlanc, bought the inn, a transaction which, perhaps unwisely, they concluded on Friday the thirteenth. One of the first waitresses they hired refused to go down in the basement for supplies because, she said, she was psychic and a presence named Cyrus was down there.

"We pooh-poohed it and laughed," says Angela LeBlanc, "but she was very, very serious."

Then the LeBlancs heard the story of Silas and put two and two together (after all, "Cyrus" sounds like "Silas"). Silas confirmed the story by making three carved mugs levitate in the bar and crash into the back of the barman's head, an incident Angela LeBlanc might have found difficult to believe if she hadn't been in the bar when it happened.

"That kind of made a believer out of me," she says.

Since then, present owners Alex and Kathy Pratt have heard inexplicable banging noises, like someone knocking on a wall in the inn at night. Then Alex Pratt was in the bar with two other people when he saw someone walk into the restaurant. He went in to see who it was and found the room was empty.

"I even looked under the tablecloths," he says, "but there was no one hiding."

Perhaps he was wise not to ask too many questions. A waitress who boasted on her last night in the restaurant that the ghost "never got me" could only watch in amazement as a glass on her tray promptly rose up into the air of its own accord, then smashed to the floor.

KENNEBUNK INN

"If there's a spirit at the inn, it's nothing to worry about," Pratt says. "He's not a malignant presence."

No, but mischievous, maybe. He gets blamed for many things, including the embarrassing collapse of a honeymooning couple's bed in Room 8. A reporter from the *Boston Globe* who spent the night in that room found it an uneventful visit. But on the other hand, a group of amateur ghost hunters who made some tape recordings in the silent cellar were amazed to find later that their tape was full of mysterious ticking noises. So perhaps old Silas is still checking the books and composing the occasional ode in the silence of the long, dark nights.

KENNEBUNK INN

Address:	45 Main Street, U.S. 1, Kennebunk, Maine 04043
Telephone:	(207) 985-3351, or for information and reservations (800) 743-1799
Facilities:	Award-winning cuisine, pub
Price Range:	Inexpensive to moderate

RANGELEY INN

Rangeley, Maine

POISED BETWEEN the forests and mountains of Maine and the six Rangeley Lakes, the Rangeley Inn is a turn-of-the-century country inn with authentically restored rooms and antiques. It is open all year, catering to everyone from summer sun-seekers to winter sports enthusiasts. Despite Rangeley's relative solitude, it is a lively spot.

The rooms in the old building are attractive, and they all have private bathrooms. Some come complete with whirlpool baths and even open fireplaces. The lobby has a roaring fire in season, too. There is a large dining room, a lounge featuring live entertainment, and a veranda-style porch where guests can find a comfortable chair overlooking Main Street. Motel-style accommodation is available in a separate building behind the inn.

Some guests believe that the inn, although not expensive, is overpriced for what it offers. But it should be emphasized that the modified American plan (lodging, plus dinner and breakfast from the complete menu) is available on a per-person basis. The food is plentiful and good.

With live entertainment in the pub on weekends, the Rangeley Inn knows how to keep the majority of its guests happy, especially its winter skiers. It can accommodate up to 110 people at any one time in its fifty bedrooms.

THE GHOST at Rangeley Inn is Clarence. At least, that's the name that innkeepers Fay and Ed Carpenter have given to the friendly spirit who seems to be around to help out whenever there is a crisis.

Clarence first stepped in about twenty years ago when the Carpenters had just held an emergency meeting to decide how to deal with a staffing crisis in the kitchen. They came out of the meeting to find "a young lady standing in our kitchen. She looked like a hippie, with a long skirt of coarse fabric, boots, and long braid of hair. She seemed pleasant enough." The Carpenters were not quite sure how she had gotten into the house, let alone where she had come from. But she offered to wash up, was given a job, and remained at the inn for the rest of the season.

"While this incident was only a little surprising then, it was to be repeated time and again," say the Carpenters. "An urgent need, followed by the appearance of someone with the necessary skill to fill this need very capably, just in the nick of time."

Eventually, the Carpenters began to wonder whether they, or the inn, were being looked after by a sort of trainee guardian angel, like Clarence in *It's a Wonderful Life*. That's how Clarence got his name.

"We have decided it's Clarence who makes the floors squeak and the radiators sing at odd times, when the mood takes him," Ed Carpenter says. "We have tried to make him comfy, along with all our guests. In this case, though, Rangeley Inn appears to be his home."

The Carpenters add that their only regret is that Clarence is too shy to put in a public appearance. But he might have. Photographer Tony Hudson, on assignment in the lovely Rangeley Lakes region in 1984, had an odd experience in the small hours after the noise from some sort of celebration downstairs echoed in his room until 1:00 A.M.

Things quieted down, and he dozed off. Expecting to be called early to take photographs of a herd of moose at sunrise, he was awakened at 2:00 A.M. when somebody came into his room. At first he thought it was the boatman. But when the figure didn't speak, he decided it must be a lost late-night reveler. He muttered, "Haven't you noisy blighters left yet?" The figure did leave by fading silently into the woodwork.

The Carpenters were unabashed by this incident. Indeed, they are still a trifle indignant that anyone should think caring Clarence would ever do such a thing to disturb a guest.

RANGELEY INN

Address:	P.O. Box 160, Rangeley, Maine 04970
Telephone:	(207) 864-3341, or for reservations (800) MOMENTS
Fax:	(207) 864-3634
Facilities:	Live entertainment, conferences and banquets
Price Range:	Inexpensive

MARYLAND

ANGELS IN THE ATTIC

North Beach, Maryland

THE "ANGELS" which give this unique bed-and-breakfast its name are everywhere: a collection of guardian angels and Victorian cherubs which turn up all around the building, sometimes in the most surprising places.

Built in 1903, and later named West Lawn Inn by the owners then, Angels in the Attic is one of the original guesthouses in Calvert County. Inns flourished here when North Beach and Chesapeake Beach were popular resort destinations for people coming from the Baltimore/Washington, D.C., area to escape the summer heat.

Innkeepers Denise England Devoe and Linda Chappelaar Travers have lovingly renovated this North Beach landmark, just one block from the famed Chesapeake Bay and Beach. It comes complete with white picket fence and the original hardwood floors and windows, at the heart of the beach community.

The building is air conditioned and has ten guest bedrooms, three with private baths. Each room is individually decorated and contains turn-of-the-century furnishings. Public rooms include a large sun room, a formal living room with delightful murals, and an upstairs tea room. Cable TV, a cassette player, a piano, and books and games are there to be enjoyed. Breakfast is buffet style, and described as "expanded continental." There is a no-smoking rule.

Besides being a bed-and-breakfast, Angels in the Attic specializes in Victorian afternoon teas, offered throughout the year to the public. The Yuletide tea, Victorian Christmas tea, and Valentine's tea are three popular winter events. Angels in the Attic is also the setting for exciting murder mystery weekends, when guests face the challenge of solving fun-filled "whodunits" in a suitably atmospheric setting.

THE GHOST at Angels in the Attic is presumed to be Elsie Chambers, a former innkeeper.

The inn was built in 1903 as a guest house and has always served in that capacity. Denise Devoe and Linda Travers bought it in 1992 and began alterations to increase the number of bedrooms. During construction, Devoe and her daughter moved into the property and began to notice a whole series of unexplained occurrences. Doors and dresser drawers opened and shut by themselves. An old armoire, left locked because of a lost key, was one day found open.

The changes to the house included creating a new door the ghost didn't seem to like. When the carpet fitter arrived, an unseen hand slammed the door shut in front of him. The carpet fitter was so frightened that he ran off and refused to finish the job.

Most mysteriously of all, there was a knock on the dining room door one day in 1922. Devoe opened it to find herself confronted by a disheveled old man carrying a newspaper.

"Elsie's back," announced the old man, without any preamble. "The lace curtains are up, so I know she's back. I painted seventeen rooms for her, all in different colors."

Devoe explained that he must be mistaken. Nobody named Elsie lived there, she said, and turned him away. Then, realizing that the stranger might be able to enlighten her about the house's history, she quickly opened the door again and went outside to look for him. But the old man had disappeared.

This odd incident prompted Devoe to research the inn's history, and she soon discovered that the property had indeed been owned and operated by someone named Elsie Chambers.

If Elsie gives the Angels in the Attic a touch of romance and mystery, however, she cannot take credit for its name.

"It has nothing to do with Elsie's presence," Devoe says. "I picked it long before opening the inn. I collect angels for my Christmas tree."

Rather more prosaically, her partner liked the idea because the word "Angels" would mean that the inn would find a place near the front of the phone book.

"We weren't entirely sure about the name at first," Devoe says. "But now it seems very fitting."

ANGELS IN THE ATTIC

Address:	9200 Chesapeake Avenue, P.O. Box 70, North Beach, Maryland 20714
Telephone:	(301) 855-2607 or (800) 260-1212
Facilities:	Special afternoon teas and mystery weekends
Price Range:	Inexpensive

THE BLUE MAX INN

Chesapeake City, Maryland

THIS COMFORTABLE bed-and-breakfast owes its name to author Jack Hunter, whose World War 1 flying saga *The Blue Max* has made thrilling reading and viewing for millions of people.

Hunter, a past owner of this delightful 1850s property, has one of the house's principal guest bedrooms named after him, a room of charm and distinction opening on to a private veranda.

It was this, and the other verandas of this Georgian federal home, that earned the nickname "the house with generous porches." Whether overlooking the shady street or the pretty gardens, they make an ideal spot for relaxing. One is glassed, a sunny spot where guests can enjoy the hearty breakfast served by innkeeper Philip Braeunig. This meal is also served in the formal dining room with its great fireplace. Afternoon tea at the Blue Max is something of an occasion, too, served English style.

All seven guest rooms are finished with the same flair as the Hunter Room, decorated in individual styles reflecting the very best of Victoriana, but with all the modern comforts and amenities that one might expect, including unique tubs.

Chesapeake City—once logged on the map as "the Village of Bohemia"—is a center for water sports of all kinds. This is also horse country, and there are special tours of the area available for enthusiasts. If you prefer bargain hunting, then a visit to one of the two auction sales held locally each week is a must. There is a factory outlet mall nearby.

THE GHOST at The Blue Max is a Dr. Conrey, who lived at the house when it was still known by the name of the family who built it, the Lindseys (owners of the local sawmill). He now has a delightful room named after him at the inn.

Conrey's life was not all sunshine. His troubles—not documented, but apparently extreme—eventually overcame him. He committed suicide in his apartment on the third floor.

Since then, he has been sensed by many guests, his spirit still occupying the rooms he made his own during his lifetime.

Braeunig says *he* has not come across the doctor. But he has heard so many reports of a strange presence from his guests, there can be no doubt that Conrey is still enjoying the hospitality of The Blue Max.

THE BLUE MAX INN

Address:	300 Bohemia Avenue, P.O. Box 30, Chesapeake City, Maryland 21915
Telephone:	(410) 885-2781
Fax:	(410) 885 2809
Facilities:	Solarium, gardens
Price Range:	Moderate

BOHEMIA HOUSE

Chesapeake City, Maryland

OVERLOOKING THE RIVER from which it takes its name, Bohemia House has its origins in colonial times. The first owner of the land was Kitty Knight, instrumental in saving Georgetown from the British in the Revolutionary War. She was awarded the property by George Washington for "services rendered."

Almost a century later, Knight's descendants set about building their homestead on a knoll overlooking the lovely lower reaches of the Bohemia River and Town Point, now encompassed by the growth of Chesapeake City. These descendants of the eighteenth-century heroine chose to erect a sturdy fieldstone mansion with the outward appearance of a whimsical Victorian-Italianate villa.

This part of Maryland's eastern shore is horse country, and present owners Herbert and Sally Worsley have taken the sport as a decorative scheme for their warmly welcoming bed-and-breakfast.

There is a massive stewards' bench from the Coney Island Racetrack in the main hall, surrounded with all kinds of equine memorabilia: horsey prints and pictures abound in the rooms. This all blends with antique furniture, drapes, and objets d'art that make for a comfortable and interesting stay, in an atmosphere of "Thoroughbred" nostalgia.

The back porch has lovely river views from its rocking chairs, looking out over the gardens. This is a delightfully restful spot to relax after a day's sightseeing or sports.

Horseback riding and racing apart, Bohemia is a yachting center. Marinas at Bohemia Bay and the Two Rivers Yacht Basin give on to the Bohemia River itself, and the waters of Chesapeake Bay are only a short sail away. For sightseeing excursions, Washington, D.C., is within easy reach, and the lovely coastline of Maryland makes a pleasant drive.

THE GHOST of Bohemia House is Margaret Huber, a daughter of the house in the 1920s.

For a home so steeped in history as the Bohemia House (it was an important stop on the Underground Railroad, with tunnels running through its foundations), it is surprising Margaret seems to be its only spook.

The Huber family, bakers in Philadelphia, willed the house to their only daughter, Margaret. She and her husband lived there through the long days of Prohibition. But they were a couple who loved to enjoy themselves and a little moonshine, too. They gave lively and very noisy parties almost every night.

During one rather riotous party, Margaret disappeared. She was last seen with her husband during a heated argument. Next day, there was no sign of her. Nor has there been any sign of her since, at least in tangible form. But investigations aimed at recreating Margaret's last hours suggested that, dispirited by the argument with her husband, she took her car and drove to a nearby high bridge over the river. There she parked her car and jumped to her death.

However, local gossip has always maintained that Margaret's husband was implicated in her death. An elderly neighbor, a guest at the party, suspected that Margaret, while arguing on the stairs, slipped and fell, breaking her neck. Or—his preferred theory—she was murdered by her husband in his alcoholic rage.

In either case, gossip says he then panicked, hid the body in the old Underground Railroad tunnels below the back porch, and "set up" Margaret's suicide.

His ruse seems to have succeeded, for investigations were dropped.

Not long ago, a psychic visited the Bohemia House. He immediately sensed Margaret's spirit lingering around her grave in the catacombs under the porch. He identified a mound he said contained her body. Once again, matters—and hopefully Margaret—were left to rest.

However, a woman's figure has recently begun to appear descending the staircase. She is dressed in a long white evening gown of the 1930s.

And the Worsleys have noticed strange happenings. In what was Margaret's room, now rearranged to suit the Worsleys, furniture and knickknacks are moved back to what seem to be Margaret's preferred positions. Missing pillows have reappeared spontaneously on "her" bed. And she sometimes even seems to doze there. Sally Worsley often finds an imprint of a human form on "her" side of the pretty canopied bed. And neither locks nor wedges will keep the bedroom door closed.

There are often sounds of jazz music and of a lively cocktail party, when it is otherwise tranquil. The scent of roses pervades the rooms when none are nearby—a scent usually closely followed by one of Margaret's "tricks."

But perhaps most extraordinary of all, Margaret seems to be very sensitive to arguments. If anyone starts squabbling in the house, she reminds them of her fate, slamming doors and throwing flowers at the feet of the arguing couple.

A peace offering, perhaps? Or a reminder of Bohemian days at the Bohemia House?

BOHEMIA HOUSE

Address:	1236 Town Point Road, Chesapeake City, Maryland 21915
Telephone:	(410) 885-3024
Fax:	(410) 885-2668
Facilities:	Bed and breakfast with heated swimming pool
Price Range:	Moderate

THE CASTLE

Mount Savage, Maryland

THERE'S A CORNER of the pretty little town of Mount Savage that is forever Scotland.

Some 150 years ago, Delano Roosevelt—an uncle of President Franklin D. Roosevelt—acquired the property as a base for his hobby: an ironworks (which later outgrew the estate and relocated to Pittsburgh). On the estate, Roosevelt built himself a replica of one of Scotland's picturesque stone castles, Craig Castle in the Highlands.

Today this spectacular house is a bed-and-breakfast set among richly planted, English-style gardens. Owners Bill and Andrea Myer obviously have a soft spot for things Scottish, for the house is now refurbished in Scottish baronial style with many period items, original gas lighting, and massive gas fireplaces. The library and the great hall are atmospheric places to relax or dine. The six guest bedrooms—all bearing Scottish names—have handsome four-posters or a French Empire sleigh bed.

Afternoon tea at The Castle is a high spot in any stay, and delicious homemade scones in the Scottish style are featured on the menu. Breakfasts are hearty, too.

The Castle is set high in the mountains of western Maryland, amid wooded scenery reminiscent of Craig Castle's setting in the lochs and mountains of the Scottish Highlands. Excellent hiking terrain is all around, and there is a wide range of water sports. There are a number of ski centers nearby, too. Rather less energetic is the round-trip from Cumberland to Frostburg on the Allegheny scenic train, which runs May through December.

THE GHOST at The Castle is of a Scotsman named Ramsay, a former owner.

Ramsay arrived in Mount Savage in the early 1870s. Evidently wealthy, he bought The Castle and installed his family, glad to have found a spot so like his native land.

A brickmaker by trade, Ramsay produced the first glazed bricks in America. Indeed, he loved the feel of stone of all kinds, from marble to granite. Hankering for privacy, he surrounded The Castle with a massive stone wall in the style of the great Scottish estates. Inside, he created a beautiful garden filled with statues he had shipped in from Europe.

Ramsay's life in his new home was cozy until the Wall Street crash, when his fortune disappeared almost overnight. His brickworks failed, and The Castle was repossessed by the banks to pay off his debts.

In his rage at the turn his life had taken, Ramsay rushed out into his gardens with a hammer and smashed all his precious statues, toppling them into the dust the same way his own fortunes had been toppled by fickle fate.

The newly impoverished Ramsay was forced to take a job as an ordinary laborer in a ceramics factory. Broken-hearted, he soon became ill and died. He and his wife now lie buried in Mount Savage Cemetery, in a vault made of Ramsay glazed bricks.

But the present owners of The Castle, Bill and Andrea Myer, know just how hard it was for Ramsay to leave his "little bit of Scotland." In fact, they suspect that he never really did leave.

Since the Myers moved into The Castle in 1984, they have seen and heard Ramsay. His footsteps echo around the empty third floor of The Castle, and the shadow of a man in a dark-colored frock coat has been seen there, as well as in the great hall and the library.

It is hard to dismiss this Scottish specter as "Scotch mist." The reports are so frequent, and so consistent, it seems certain Ramsay has settled back in his old home and intends to remain there forever.

THE CASTLE

Address:	Route 36, P.O. Box 578, Mount Savage, Maryland 21545
Telephone:	(301) 759-5946
Facilities:	English-style gardens
Price Range:	Inexpensive to moderate

KENT MANOR INN

Stevensville, Kent Island Estates, Maryland

SET AMONG 226 acres of park and farmland on historic Kent Island Estates, beside the blue waters of Thompson Creek, stands the lovely white-columned house that is the Kent Manor Inn.

Once the "big house" for this waterside plantation, Kent Manor dates from 1820 when it was the home of Alexander Thompson. Today, this gracious property is a flourishing hotel and restaurant where Sunday brunch in particular is a treat for locals and visitors alike.

Carefully restored to its early Victorian comfort and elegance, the inn has four dining rooms and a number of cozy lounges, some of which retain their original Italian marble fireplaces and window seats. The twenty-four guest bedrooms and suites are fastidiously furnished in keeping with the age and traditions of the building, with finely carved wooden bedsteads and other antique pieces. They all have every modern comfort as well.

The house has verandas and a glassed-in solarium overlooking Thompson Creek. The extensive grounds include no less than one and a half miles of foreshore, and contain a number of marked paths and trails for joggers. Swimming, golf, volleyball, horseshoes, and croquet are among the hotel's available sports in summer.

Nearby are a number of shopping malls, including antique shops, local crafts, and a factory outlet. There are several wildlife refuges within the radius of a few miles, and the big cities of Annapolis, Baltimore, and Washington, D.C., are all within a leisurely hour's drive.

THE GHOST at Kent Manor Inn is that of Thompson himself: old Alexander Thompson, the original owner of the plantation back in the early 1800s.

Thompson, after whom the nearby creek is named, was an extremely heavy smoker, so much so that he sometimes seemed to exist in a cloud of blue smoke.

His own bedroom, the room in which he died, is now Room 209. A century or so has passed since Thompson died, but Room 209 still carries a lingering scent of tobacco. No one is known to have smoked within its walls for years. Staff cannot eliminate the odor, no matter what they do.

Thompson seems to be the cause of some strange occurrences at the inn, too. Playful in life, he is playful still. Staff have reported being trapped in Room 209 by a table inexplicably pushed in front of the door. Lights flicker on and off for no apparent reason.

Thompson likes life to be lively. His tricks happen most often when the house is quiet. And it's when there are few people about and there is not much going on that a number of witnesses, including members of staff and two former owners, have reported seeing Thompson himself. On each occasion, he simply watches from a dim corner.

By contrast, he also enjoys a good wedding. The inn is a favorite place for celebrating marriages, and Thompson is often spotted at these ceremonies, joining in the fun as an extra, if intangible, guest.

KENT MANOR INN

Address:	500 Kent Manor Drive, Stevensville, Kent Island Estates, Maryland 21666
Telephone:	(410) 643–5757
Facilities:	Lakeside setting, solarium
Price Range:	Moderate to expensive

SNOW HILL INN

Snow Hill, Maryland

ON A PLOT of land in the very heart of the ancient township of Snow Hill, early settlers built an inn. Snow Hill, named a "royal port" on the Pocomoke River in 1693, grew; the inn was sold; and in the 1790s there arose in its stead the handsome mansion which forms the basis of today's Snow Hill Inn.

In the late 1800s the house was owned by Dr. John Adyelotte, who practiced medicine there for eighty years and who lived to age 101. The original ironwork gate bearing his name still graces the front of this attractive property. But Dr. Adyelotte and his immediate successors have used the property for a number of purposes, including a spell as the town's post office, before it once again became an inn.

Today's owners, Jim and Kathy Washington, have encouraged the inn's reputation as a good spot to dine. Its restaurant is renowned and features local seafood such as delicious Maryland blue crabs. Above the restaurant are four comfortable guest rooms, each furnished in period style and two with their own working fireplaces.

Visitors to Snow Hill will find plenty to see and do in this delightful little riverside town. There are walking tours of its historic center, full of lovely old houses and many antique shops. There are cruises on Tillie the Tug or by canoe along the waterway, the banks of which are a nature preserve and bird-watcher's paradise.

Farther afield, the resorts of Ocean City and Assateague Island are within a half-hour's drive; the beautiful state parks of Shad Landing and Milburn Landing are nearby; and there are no less than eight challenging golf courses in the locality. Baltimore, Washington, D.C., and Philadelphia are little more than one hundred miles distant.

THE GHOST at Snow Hill is J. J., the son of the local doctor who once lived in the inn.

Jay J. Adyelotte, son of the Dr. Adyelotte whose name is still on the front gate, was a student in Baltimore in the 1920s. The boy's studies got to be too much for him, and he took his own life.

It is only since the present innkeepers, the Washingtons, took charge of the house about six years ago that J. J. has made his presence felt in his former home. Strange things suddenly started to happen around the two-hundred-year-old property.

Construction workers, helping to renovate the house, were asked to repair an upstairs window. No matter what they tried, nothing short of a sledgehammer would shift the stubborn sash window. This in itself spooked the team of hefty young builders. But they got an even greater shock when the window suddenly flew open unaided. The construction team, who had been staying at the inn while they worked on it, demanded to be moved to another hotel.

Shortly after the inn reopened, the Washingtons themselves experienced J. J.'s tricks: playing with a roll of tinfoil in the kitchen as though it were a drumstick and habitually lighting the candles in the dining room.

Guests assigned to the bedroom with the reluctant window have come face-to-face with J. J. Besides reporting inexplicable noises coming from the room, such as a door slamming when there is no one around, people have spotted a slight, fair-haired young man standing beside the stubborn window and smiling.

And yes, a photograph of Jay J. Adyelotte taken just before his death shows him to have been a slightly built, smiling, fair-haired young man.

SNOW HILL INN

Address:	104 E. Market Street, Snow Hill, Maryland 21863
Telephone:	(410) 632-2102
Facilities:	Seafood restaurant, gourmet picnics
Price Range:	Inexpensive

SPRING BANK FARM

Frederick, Maryland

ONE HUNDRED YEARS to the day after the cornerstone of Spring Bank Farm was laid, the present owners, Ray and Beverly Compton, moved in.

The house the Comptons acquired was in a far different state from the elegant Graeco-Italian villa created by gentleman farmer George Houck in 1880. On completion it was reported in the local newspaper to contain "all the modern improvements that judiciously expended wealth could obtain or refined taste suggest." But when the Comptons bought the property, it was derelict, populated only by a family of raccoons in the reading room, wild beehives in the wainscot, and a breeding colony of grackles in the bedrooms.

This beautiful mansion has been fully restored as a no-smoking house. Furnishings and decor include stunning original friezes and stenciled ceilings retouched to their former vivid color. The drawing room, library, and seven guest bedrooms are furnished with period pieces such as carved armoires, canopied beds, and a multitude of other items culled from the stock of Ray Compton's antique shop. There are tall ormolu mirrors, brass lamps, fine etched-glass panels, and even a billiard room reflecting a remarkably feminine style, with panels of fruit, bird, and flower motifs on its walls. The hallway is hung with tooled leather.

Breakfasts of seasonal fruits and home baking are served in guests' bedrooms or on the verandas: laden trays set with fine china, a different pattern every day.

Views from the belvedere on top of the house are superb, out over the open, rolling Maryland countryside. The Comptons are keen bicyclers and will happily point out the specially marked trails in the area. The Appalachian Trail runs nearby, and the countryside is ideal for walking and riding. Visitor attractions include the Catocin Mountain Zoo (the president's Camp David is among these hills); the town of Frederick itself, home to Francis Scott Key, some of whose memorabilia are housed in its museum; and Rose Hill Manor, home to the state's first governor and now a lively museum for children.

SPRING BANK FARM

THE GHOST of Spring Bank Farm is Tilly, daughter of the house's first owner, George Houck.

Tilly died in the house at age thirty-three. The cause of her death is not recorded in Frederick's cemetery records.

She was one of five children and was devoted to her mother, a frail, permanently ailing woman, whom Tilly nursed with devotion. A local historian who knew the house as a child, now a centenarian, is certain that Tilly haunts Spring Bank. He says she haunts it because she died before her mother and feels guilty about deserting her.

Another theory enjoying local support is that Tilly's haunting is designed to track down the murderer of her best friend, nicknamed Hollerin' Kate.

Whatever the reason for Tilly's clinging to Spring Bank, it seems she still wants to care for guests. Owner Beverly Compton's sister met Tilly when staying in Tilly's former bedroom, with her own daughter. She awoke during the night to see a young woman wearing a burgundy-colored gown, with a corsage of flowers and her hair in a bun, bending over the bed. As Compton's sister stirred, the figure disappeared. Her daughter saw and felt nothing.

[122]

The Comptons themselves have seen and heard nothing of Tilly. But they have researched the Houck family to recreate the house's original glories wherever possible.

Tilly has made her presence felt to both resident and potential guests. One young man, planning his wedding reception at the house, was taken aback as he entered Tilly's room. A total skeptic until that moment, he said he was sure it held the ghost of a young woman. He had never had such a feeling before.

Tilly's appearances are few and far between. Guests in her former home might find that their closest encounter with her is when they browse among the paintings hanging throughout the house, some of which were brought back to the Comptons by a great-granddaughter of George Houck. Two of the dimly colorful old oil paintings are signed "Tilly."

SPRING BANK FARM

Address:	7945 Worman's Mill Road, Frederick, Maryland 21701
Telephone:	(301) 694-0440
Facilities:	Bed-and-breakfast in tranquil setting, billiards
Price Range:	Moderate

COLONIAL INN

Concord, Massachusetts

FAMOUS SINCE 1716, when it was the home of one of Concord's first settlers, the Colonial Inn has become one of the town's most enduring landmarks. It overlooks historically rich Monument Square and has all the elegance of a former era.

The individually appointed guest rooms reflect the hotel's colonial style, yet offer such contemporary amenities as color TV, touch-tone telephones, and private baths. In the Main Inn, each room is individually styled and traditionally decorated. The Prescott Wing rooms have a cozy country charm. There is also the Keyes House Annex, featuring fully furnished one- and two-bedroom suites for longer stays.

A complimentary cup of coffee and newspaper for each guest starts the day, followed by breakfast in the Merchants Row restaurant. The restaurant also serves lunch and dinner, and there is a cafe for lighter snacks. Nightly entertainment and snacks are offered in one of the two lounges. The historic charm of the Thoreau Room is an intimate setting for afternoon tea.

The public areas of the inn feature several fireplaces, original woodwork, polished floors, and stacks of country charm. For colonial treasures and unique souvenirs, the John Anthony Pewter Shop is a happy-hunting ground.

The "two histories" of Concord come together to offer visitors a choice of things to see and do. There is ample Revolutionary War history at the Minute Man National Park, the Old North Bridge, and the Wright Tavern. Literary history comes to life in the Concord Museum, the Orchard House, the Old Manse, and the Wayside. For recreation in a historic setting, try boating or canoeing on the Concord River or swimming at Thoreau's Walden Pond.

THE GHOST at the Colonial Inn is believed to be Dr. Joseph Minot, a Revolutionary War surgeon born in 1726 and a life-long resident of Concord. He made his home in what is now the oldest part of the inn which houses Room 24. It's there a blushing bride spent a very strange honeymoon night on June 14, 1966.

Nothing out of the ordinary had previously been reported by guests staying in Room 24, or for that matter anywhere else in the hotel. But newlywed Judith Fellenz, from Highland Falls, New York, awoke in the middle of the night with the feeling that, besides herself and her bridegroom, there was a third presence in the room. She opened her eyes and saw a grayish figure at the side of the bed.

"It was not a distinct person, but a shadowy mass in the shape of a standing figure," she said later. "It remained still for a moment, then slowly floated to the foot of the bed in front of the fireplace. After pausing for a few seconds, the apparition slowly melted away. It was a terrifying experience."

Mrs. Fellenz was too frightened to move, let alone wake her husband. Then, when she was able to move again, her fright turned to embarrassment. Nobody would believe she had seen a ghost, she thought. Her husband bore out that fear by teasing her when she mentioned it to him. So she kept quiet about the incident until, two weeks later, she wrote to the hotel to relate what had happened and ask if they had any explanation. The curtains in Room 24 had been closed, she said, so what she saw could not have been a reflection. She was fully awake at the time she saw the "extra guest" and "certain that it was not a figment of my imagination." Her letter, which was very detailed, added, "This sounds ridiculous, but I will swear to my dying day that I have seen a ghost in your lovely inn."

The innkeeper at the time, Loring Grimes, was not as disbelieving as Mrs. Fellenz had feared and wrote back to tell her the story of Dr. Minot. He also described Concord's connections with author and philosopher Ralph Waldo Emerson, and nature lover and writer Henry David Thoreau—two other candidates for the ghost in Room 24. Mrs. Fellenz and her army officer husband were invited to make a return visit to the inn, and they did. But they stayed in a different room and saw nothing.

COLONIAL INN

Perhaps because the Fellenzes' story attracted some local press coverage, the ghost of Room 24 achieved a certain notoriety. Other guests began to describe strange experiences, and in 1986 a businesswoman from Virginia fled the hotel claiming she too had seen the ghost and would never again go anywhere near Room 24. In 1990, Mrs. Fellenz, by now remarried and going by the name of Cole, returned to the Colonial Inn—and Room 24—with her new husband, Bill. Although the shadowy figure did not reappear, the couple had a restless night.

"The room seemed to tease us," they said afterward. "There was something like an elusive beckoning."

Mrs. Cole added, "There is no doubt in my mind that a 'presence' has, indeed, attached itself to that beautiful corner room."

A local psychic who investigated the room in 1991 said it contained a benevolent male ghost who lingered there, not because of any special connection with Room 24, but because the inn was built over what had once been his lookout spot for guarding munitions. Later research disclosed that there had been a munitions dump opposite the hotel site in the early 1700s.

Also in 1991, a couple staying in Room 24 complained of being kept awake by repeated rapping noises on the inside of the adjoining bathroom door. The noises stopped whenever they went into the bathroom. But the couple were skeptics and refused to believe they might have had a visit from Minot. Many other unusual incidents that have been reported to hotel staff go unrecorded, says room sales manager Phyllis Dougherty.

As the Colonial Inn's fame has spread, so have the theories about the origins of the ghost. Emerson is a popular choice, because his family once owned the land where the inn now stands. Thoreau is known to have loved Concord dearly, so it is easy to imagine him being reluctant to leave. And Native Americans are not forgotten: One theory holds that the ghost is an angry woman from the Assabet tribe, who sold six square miles of land to the colonists so they could build Concord and who is now dissatisfied with the deal.

But no one will convince Carol McCabe that the ghost is anyone but Minot. On the night of December 9, 1994, during the most recent "sighting," he cured her stomachache.

Carol McCabe and her husband, Jim, who were staying in Room 24, had a large dinner that evening. Carol awoke at 2:45 A.M. with a stomachache. She went into the bathroom, got a glass of water, then went back to bed and lay on her stomach, "calling for the spirit of Dr. Minot."

Her SOS seems to have been answered. As Carol McCabe relates, "I suddenly felt a tingling sensation through my whole body. I felt as if electricity was going through me, and my body was rigid."

Unable to move, she could not look around to see what was causing this, but when the sensation disappeared after a few seconds, she was able to look around.

"There was nothing in the room," she says.

Then the tingling sensation and partial paralysis began again, and after it was over it was repeated a third time. As the sensations grew weaker, Carol was able to relax and finally sleep.

"I can't help but wonder if Dr. Minot not only made his presence known to me, but somehow eased my stomachache," she says.

"Unsettling, but not unpleasant," is how Mrs. McCabe describes her experience. The most noteworthy thing about the unseen guest in Room 24 of the Colonial Inn seems to be that he seldom frightens visitors. Indeed, the room is the most popular in the hotel, and is usually booked up for months ahead.

"We do believe our ghost is a friendly spirit," Phyllis Dougherty says. "Nothing bad has ever happened."

COLONIAL INN

Address:	48 Monument Square, Concord, Massachusetts 01742-1899
Telephone:	(508) 369-9200, or for reservations (800) 370-9200
Fax:	(508) 369-2170
Facilities:	History relived in luxurious surroundings
Price Range:	Moderate

DEERFIELD INN

Deerfield, Massachusetts

DEERFIELD INN, which was built in 1884, was remodeled in 1981 after a fire. It stands in what is called simply "the Street," described as the loveliest street in New England. It is now a full-service country inn, with twenty-three rooms named after people connected with the history of the village. The inn is open all year and accessible to the disabled.

The bedrooms (thirteen double rooms and ten with twin beds) have private bathrooms, individual air conditioning and telephones, and are furnished with period antiques. At the time of this writing, all were being equipped with TV sets.

Overnight guests enjoy a hearty country breakfast. Lunch and dinner also are served in the award-winning restaurant. The menus, featuring fresh local produce, change monthly and offer excellent value; there is an extensive wine list. Afternoon tea is available.

Old Deerfield is a national historic landmark. First settled in 1670, it witnessed the 1704 Indian massacre and the trials and tribulations of the American Revolution. Yet the eighteenth-century townscape seems untouched by the passage of time. No less than thirteen museum houses now line the Street and encapsulate the cultural history, art, and craftsmanship of the Pioneer Valley.

There is a wonderful arts museum in nearby Williamstown. The historic villages of Shelburne Falls and Amherst are worth visiting, antique shopping is excellent, and country walks (to the old Native American lookout spot known as the Rock) and boating trips (to see the eagles at the Barton Cove) are recommended. In winter there is cross-country skiing in Northfield and downhill skiing on Mount Tom, both about a twenty-minute drive away.

THE GHOST—or rather ghosts—at Deerfield Inn are those of a former owner, Cora Carlisle, and a rather mysterious, poltergeist-like apparition who goes by the name of Herschel.

Cora Carlisle was a great believer in spiritualism. She used to hold séances in her living room; it has since been turned into a guest room bearing her name. The spirit she sought to contact was that of her husband, John. They had worked together closely on business matters during his lifetime, and Cora wished to continue consulting him about business. She called in a medium and believed she was successful in getting through to her late husband. Local historians say that the inn became a center for spiritualist activity.

Perhaps it still is, for occasionally Cora can be heard knocking on the door of her former living room and saying, "It's Cora, let me in," in an astringent and bossy voice. Present-day occupants who open the door and peep out might spot Cora in her nightclothes, moving off smartly down the corridor.

But Cora is quite well behaved compared to Herschel.

"Herschel likes to bother the guests in Room 148, the Chester Harding Room," innkeepers Jane and Karl Sabo report. "We don't know why he's called Herschel. He's had that name before Lucille Henry, the receptionist, began working here, and she's been here for over thirty years."

There's no polite knocking on the door from Herschel.

"He slips under the door and appears in a bright box of light like a phone booth," the Sabos say. "The light breaks up and bounces around the room for a bit. If you are not paying attention by then, Herschel starts to tease by tugging at the bedclothes and lobbing magazines around the room."

A mysterious light source trying to remove the bedclothes would catch most people's attention. It proved a memorable experience for California surgeon Alan Tobias and his wife, Judith, when they vacationed in New England in May 1993. The locked door of Room 148 kept unlocking itself, static electricity cracked around the ceiling,

DEERFIELD INN

magazines were thrown around, and the bedclothes kept being pulled off the bed. At first, Alan and Judith each thought the other was playing tricks, but when they realized that neither was responsible, they tried to think of a scientific explanation for what was happening. That didn't work. The couple—who tried ringing security in vain and were reluctant to get out of bed—had to put up with what they described as the "playing" until first light. Entering into the "spirit" of the occasion, they tried singing the theme song from *Ghostbusters*, but it had no effect.

"Something was going on that I can't explain," Dr. Tobias said. The couple said they were not frightened by the experience, just "dumbfounded."

When she heard the Tobiases' story next morning, receptionist Lucille Henry said, "This is one of the bigger stories." She has heard many strange tales during her thirty years there, but neither she nor the Sabos has ever seen a ghost.

In fact, despite her guests' strange experience, Jane Sabo doesn't even believe in ghosts, although she says, "I believe you can pick up a feeling in a place where a great trauma has occurred."

One problem, however, is that according to desk clerk Tim Cronin, who has been researching the history of the 112-year-old Deerfield Inn, no great tragedies have ever been recorded there. Local folklore expert Donald Friary, the director of Old Deerfield, agrees. But both Cronin and a former nightwatchman at the hotel have heard inexplicable noises in the hotel at night, and a security guard once quit after claiming he had seen a ghost.

The Tobiases' story, which received widespread press coverage in New England, brought the Deerfield Inn a surge of bookings, although the Sabos have moved to discourage ghost-hunters armed with cameras and other such equipment. No guests canceled their bookings, but a honeymoon couple who read the Tobiases' story did ask if they could be reserved a room without Herschel.

If anything, Jan and Karl Sabo are as upset by such slights to Herschel as they would be by anyone trying to avoid their own two youngsters.

"Herschel's not a scary spirit at all," they said indignantly. "He's more like a mischievous child bothering his parents on Christmas morning and trying to get them out of bed."

DEERFIELD INN

Address:	The Street, Deerfield, Massachusetts 01342
Telephone:	(413) 774-5587
Facilities:	Historic setting, excellent restaurant
Price Range:	Inexpensive to moderate

HAWTHORNE HOTEL

Salem, Massachusetts

SALEM, A CHARMING seaport on the coast of rural Massachusetts, is a town glowing with civic pride. Its seventeenth-century houses are beautifully preserved; its parks, gardens, old churches, and fine shops are all redolent of the gracious 1800s.

The Hawthorne Hotel is high-profile proof of Salem's civic sensitivity. It rose on a patch of land on the corner of Salem Common to become the focus of the town's hospitality activities. And it was funded by a highly unusual public subscription. Such funding is often a recipe for disaster or at best mediocrity. But this particular municipal building has avoided those pitfalls and earned its place among the nation's top hotels.

An atmospheric building dating from 1920, the Hawthorne is named for a famous son of Salem, author Nathaniel Hawthorne. The hotel prides itself on its exceptional warmth of welcome, its high degree of comfort, and its gracious hospitality.

The eighty-nine guest rooms come complete with fine oak furniture, four-poster beds, and New England antiques. The public rooms include Nathaniel's Restaurant, offering local seafood and the best of American cuisine. Open fires warm the hotel's Tavern on the Green, a comfortable retreat.

As a base for following Salem's Heritage Trail, the hotel is perfectly placed. All the sights of Salem are within a few blocks—museums, churches, and other historical buildings reflecting the rather spooky Salem of the seventeenth century, when the town became notorious as the witch-hunting capital of the world. The delightful colonial city of Boston is on the doorstep, as is the lovely Massachusetts seashore.

THE GHOST of the Hawthorne Hotel is no single specter. It is in fact the all-pervading atmosphere of those grim days in the 1690s when Salem Common—and the land on which the Hawthorne Hotel now stands—was the focus of the dreadful witch-hunts that raged through this, the oldest continuous Protestant society in America.

The story is terrifying.

Through the influence of Tituba, a West Indian slave, the family of the Reverend Samuel Parris, of nearby Danvers, became notorious, and the local townships were rocked by hysteria and hate, strange phenomena, and accusations of devil worship and witchcraft.

The young girls of the Parris household were fascinated by Tituba's tales and giggled like any other young girls over the slave's stories of love, death, and voodoo from her Caribbean home.

In the simple, God-fearing society of the time, any personal vanity, any simple pleasure such as dancing, any physical handicap, or even an irreverent sense of humor or a favorite pet, could be interpreted as an insult to the Lord. Cross your neighbor and you could find yourself denounced as consorting with Satan.

Malicious gossip, spiced with Tituba's gift for charms and love potions, and spiked by the overworked imaginations of a handful of teenagers, began what became a remorseless hunt to eradicate evil and the influence of the devil from Salem.

Neighbor was suspicious of neighbor; natural phenomena were misinterpreted and misreported; spite took a hand. First accused was Rebecca Nurse, whose clapboard homestead still stands in Salem. Nurse was hanged, despite a petition by forty of her friends, many of whom later also stood condemned. Finally, an inquisitor was brought in to try the accused.

By the end of those dark days in 1692, almost 200 people had been accused and tried for witchcraft, 150 were jailed, and 19 died by hanging on Salem's Gallows Hill. One man, Giles Corey, refused to confess and died, pressed to death by great stones in an attempt to force him to recant.

"I petition to your honor," Mary Esty said, in her last words before being hanged in September 1692, "not for my own life, for I know I must die, but that no more innocent blood must be shed."

For all of Salem's bright, fresh paint, and flowers nowadays, there is a shadow still hanging over it. Salem's city fathers have carefully preserved as many records, buildings, and artifacts relating to this dark time as possible. The Salem Witch Museum is just one of the visitor attractions focusing on the witch trials, and it offers a dramatic, multisensory presentation of the events of 1692, designed to enable visitors to "witness the awesome, ominous truth." Specters rise; Tituba goes into a trance; courtroom rhetoric and hysteria abound; the Salem witches meet their fate.

The town is also known as the Halloween capital of the United States, with an annual festival celebrating everything that goes bump in the night.

But lest it seem as if the Salem of today has turned the tragic events of 1692 into a brash tourist attraction, it should be said that the town is at a focal point of much of America's early history. Its narrow lanes look much as they did in the seventeenth century. And it does have its own, very special atmosphere.

No one knows exactly where Tituba conducted her voodoo rituals, or where Salem's "witches" were buried. Nor is it known why the land by Salem Common beneath the Hawthorne Hotel remained undeveloped for some four hundred years.

HAWTHORNE HOTEL

Address:	On The Common, Salem, Massachusetts 01970
Telephone:	(508) 774-4080 or (800) SAY-STAY
Fax:	(508) 745-9842
Facilities:	In the heart of historic Salem, exercise suite
Price Range:	Expensive

LONGFELLOW'S WAYSIDE INN

Sudbury, Massachusetts

THE WAYSIDE INN, witness to almost three hundred years of American history, was initially a two-room dwelling on the Boston Post Road. It grew over the centuries to meet the demands of both the How family, who owned it, and travelers at a time when local laws dictated that an inn must "provide for a man, his horses, and his cattle."

For centuries, townspeople gathered at the inn to discuss the issues of the day. Here, too, Colonel Ezekiel How conferred with members of the Boston Committee of Safety and prepared for events that led to the birth of the United States.

Today's visitor to the Wayside Inn can enjoy the same peace and tranquillity described by Henry Wadsworth Longfellow in the prelude to his poem *Tales of a Wayside Inn*. And the Hows' tradition of hospitality continues with magnificent New England fare. Ten guest rooms are furnished with antiques, and all have private baths, telephones, and air conditioning. Indeed, tradition is such that the inn can still look after your horses in the barn across the street, although they're not sure about your cattle. The dining room is open for all meals.

After the publication of Longfellow's poem in 1863, describing the inn "built in the old colonial day, when man lived in a grander way," the inn became known as Longfellow's Wayside Inn. It is now a non-profit and educational trust. The original trust was established by Henry Ford in 1946. After a disastrous fire in 1956, Longfellow's Wayside Inn was restored with a Ford Foundation grant. The Inn is a national historic site, administered by an unpaid board of trustees. Revenue from the property helps pay for its upkeep and continuing restoration.

There are self-guided walking tours of the property, with its fourteen historic rooms and adjacent buildings, such as Ford's Martha-Mary Chapel and the Redstone School of "Mary Had a Little Lamb" fame. Boston is eleven miles away.

THE GHOSTS of Longfellow's Wayside Inn are the countless Native Americans who lie in the Indian burial site over which the original property was constructed. Although they are never seen, the site does have a slightly desolate feeling.

But perhaps it should also have a sense of hope and reconciliation, in view of Longfellow's best-known epic poem, *The Song of Hiawatha*. Written in 1855, Hiawatha tells the true story of a Mohawk chief from northern New York State who was a reformer, preached unity among the Indian tribes, and helped to form the Iroquois League. Hiawatha's love for Minnehaha—or "Laughing Water"—is well known. His statesmanship is less well known.

LONGFELLOW'S WAYSIDE INN

Address: Wayside Inn Road (off the Boston Post Road Route 20), Sudbury, Massachusetts 01776
Telephone: (508) 443-1776
Facilities: America's oldest inn, bed-and-breakfast steeped in history
Price Range: Inexpensive

VICTORIAN INN

Edgartown, Massachusetts

THIS ATTRACTIVE INN is a restored whaling captain's home in historical Edgartown on Martha's Vineyard. The traditions, charms, and ambiance of the mid-nineteenth century are maintained in the Victorian Inn and Edgartown as a whole.

Situated on lovely South Water Street, where many sea captains built their mansions, the Victorian Inn is directly across from the famous Pagoda Tree, one block above the town dock and harbor. Fine restaurants, quaint shops, museums, and art galleries are all just a short stroll away.

The inn's flower-filled guest bedrooms, some with queen- or king-sized beds, some with four-posters, have private bathrooms. The bedrooms are tastefully decorated and filled with family furniture and cherished antiques. Some of the rooms have balconies overlooking the harbor or the English garden.

The English garden is where the inn's "gourmet breakfast" is served, weather permitting. Alternatively, guests dine in the breakfast room. The inn operates a no-smoking policy.

The choice of activities on the island is enormous: tennis, golf, bicycling, horseback riding, sailing, fishing, summer theater shows, wildlife sanctuaries, and swimming or sunbathing on what are claimed to be the most beautiful and unspoiled beaches in the East.

If you want to take your car across to Martha's Vineyard, advance booking is necessary on the year-round ferry from Woods Hole. Call the Steamship Authority at (508) 477-8600. There is free parking at the Victorian Inn. But cars may also be left in attended lots around Woods Hole.

THE GHOST at the Victorian Inn is a tall, tanned, clean-shaven gentleman with a mane of silver hair and a taste for the ladies. But according to the old stories and more up-to-date resorts, this old house, built in 1857 by Captain Lafayette Rowley, also contains an entire cast of restless spirits.

The star of the show is undoubtedly the silver-haired man, who first put in an appearance at the inn when a couple returned to their room late at night, after a meal and pub crawl in Edgartown. The couple went to bed, but the man awoke an hour or two later with chest pains which he immediately put down to indigestion. When he opened his eyes, however, he found that the cause of the discomfort was a Victorian gentleman who appeared to be sitting on his chest. He was wearing a black, high-collared frock coat, his hair was brushed back, and he had an angular face and slightly sneering expression.

Dismissing the apparition as imagination, the guest went back to sleep. When he awoke in the morning, however, the memory of the incident still fresh in his mind, he got a very nasty shock. His wife stirred beside him, opened her eyes, and said, "I had the oddest dream in the night. I dreamt I woke up and there was a man sitting on your chest."

Not long ago a woman from New York apparently confronted the same tall, silver-maned spook. She awoke when her bedroom's balcony door blew open and the man strode into the room. Walking over to her bed, he reached out, and firmly tweaked one of her nipples. Then he glided off.

Rather more alarming was a gang of five rough-looking seagoing characters who appeared briefly outside guests' rooms, then vanished. In other cases, furniture was thrown into the hall during the night. And in one empty room, items of furniture were wedged up against the doors from the inside, so nobody could get in. These incidents moved former owner Kathy Appert to stage a short exorcism ceremony, which seemed to quiet down the spirit activity. Certainly, the gang of cut-throats disappeared. The romantic wraith with a penchant for chests of all kinds hasn't been seen for some years, either.

Stephen Caliri, who has been the innkeeper since 1993, says, "My wife and I have only heard and read about the many stories regarding the ghosts of the inn. We have had our share of lights turning on, doors unlocking, appliances turning on by themselves; and, of course, in a big old house lots of things go bump in the night. But this skeptic has little to add personally to the tales of the Victorian Inn."

This has been a bit of a disappointment to the majority of the guests, who know the inn's haunted reputation and are surprised to find the ghosts in a bashful mood. After all, the Victorian Inn is still a regular stop for tourists taking the resort's popular "Haunted Edgartown" tour, so it has something to live up to.

But things could be improving for ghost-hunters. "Most of our ghost stories have involved the inn's third floor rooms—the most recently renovated," Caliri says. "However, as work has progressed and renovations are now mostly on the second floor, the frequency of reports coming from those rooms is on the rise."

So, who knows what will come out of the woodwork next? As Caliri admits, "It would appear that our ghosts don't approve of change, even for the better."

VICTORIAN INN

Address:	P.O. Box 947, 24 South Water Street, Edgartown, Massachusetts 02539
Telephone:	(508) 627-4784
Facilities:	Charming bed-and-breakfast on island of Martha's Vineyard
Price Range:	Moderate

MISSISSIPPI

HARBOUR OAKS INN

Pass Christian, Mississippi

HARBOUR OAKS INN, opposite the Pass Christian yacht harbor and the beach, is the only remaining hotel from an era when "the Pass" was an internationally known resort and the Gulf Coast was known as the American Riviera. A three-story building with covered porches on the first and second floors, the inn has a number of beautifully furnished rooms, let on a bed-and-breakfast basis.

All the rooms have a double bed and private bathroom, with the master suite boasting a Jacuzzi. Besides the fine furnishings, the rooms are dotted with family antiques, art, and mementos, making this a very upscale bed-and-breakfast indeed. In addition to the reception and dining parlors, a charming kitchen and a den with its own billiard table and card table are available to guests.

While the front rooms have a beach and harbor view, the back rooms overlook a deep and restful back yard filled with gigantic live oak trees strung with spanish moss. The house is listed in the *National Register of Historic Places* and, with the assistance of the Mississippi Department of Archives and History, restoration is a continuing process, although it seemed in almost perfect condition when I stayed there in 1993.

There are plenty of places to dine in Pass Christian, a charming antebellum community with some breathtaking beach-front architectural treasures. A one-time resort area for wealthy New Orleans aristocrats and southern plantation owners, it is now principally a yachting center.

But the twenty-six-mile-long beach of white sand is an attraction, as are fishing, golf (there are twenty-one golf courses along the coast), the Jefferson Davis Shrine at Beauvoir, the Marine Life Center in Gulfport, and the flourishing casinos in Biloxi. New Orleans is an easy day trip. Pass Christian contains plenty of antique shops and a flourishing artists' colony.

THE GHOST at Harbour Oaks Inn is a little girl, about ten, who has long dark hair and wears a hat. She is a playful, helpful child, much loved by some guests. She has been known to pick up sewing things dropped onto the floor of the front porch room to the left of the front door.

Many people sense the little girl's presence and describe her as warm and compassionate. Some people have suggested her mother is around, too, although both spirits, if they exist, are definitely friendly.

But the spirits at the Harbour Oaks have not always been so friendly. When proprietors Tony and Diane Brugger moved in, Diane was conscious of "a multiple male presence" on the landing and in some of the upstairs rooms, including the Bruggers' own quarters. The dogs noticed it, too.

"I would go to the top of the stairs and experience an overwhelming feeling of pressure, suffocation, hair standing on end, and would have to physically force myself over the threshold," says Diane. "The intimidating presence would never leave while I was up there."

The Bruggers and their friends named these spirits "the fellas." Even Tony Brugger, a skeptic, experienced the phenomena. Eventually, an expert was called in and, as Diane Brugger recalls, the spirits were "given the option" of leaving voluntarily or being helped on their way. The "fellas," who said they were soldiers (apparently from the Civil War when Harbour Oaks, then known as the Crescent Hotel, was used as a hospital) preferred the first option. They were gone within a week.

Not so the little girl.

"She is still here," reported Diane Brugger in mid-1995. "She makes her presence known in small ways. The 'feelings' associated with her are very compassionate: cheerful, playful, helpful, warm, and nonthreatening. Those who have experienced her feel a sense of loss when she leaves."

Tony Brugger is less forthcoming about the ghost. Still a skeptic despite his experience with "the fellas," he finds the subject embarrassing. He and his wife have often discussed the advisability of refusing to discuss the subject of ghosts with guests at all.

But for that to work, the couple would have to be sure their guests wouldn't meet the ghosts for themselves. And if my experience in 1993 is anything to go by, that's hard to guarantee.

I was traveling with a small party of friends, and three of us—my wife and I, and a woman executive from the Travel South marketing group, Carmel Modica—booked into Harbour Oaks while the rest of the group stayed elsewhere in Pass Christian.

Tired after our travels, my wife and I settled for a quiet stroll and a drink, followed by an early night. The rest of the group went out for dinner, then on to a casino. We retired early to our porch front room on the right of the front door. We were asleep when Modica returned to her room, the porch front room on the left of the front door.

We had learned the story of the little girl during the evening, but Modica didn't know she was in the haunted room. So it was with some interest that we asked her, next morning, "How did you sleep?"

"Not at all well," she replied. "There seemed to be a little girl in the room, and she was looking for something on the floor. I kept seeing a little girl and toys everywhere, but in the morning none of them were there."

She wondered whether she had downed one drink too many in the casino the night before or whether her imagination was playing tricks. When we told her the ghost story, she paled visibly.

"That's what the little girl was doing!" she exclaimed. "She was picking up sewing things and putting them on the table."

The Bruggers were not surprised when we told them what had happened, but they were still a little defensive about their ghost. As recently as spring 1995, Diane Brugger suggested, "If you want to write about ghosts, why don't you write about the Blue Rose Restaurant two doors down? Now they have a very active spirit."

Have they, indeed? By chance, I had lunched at the Blue Rose before staying at Harbour Oaks and had met the proprietor. But I neither heard nor saw the restaurant ghost. Still, all these stories do make the peaceful little gulf resort of Pass Christian an unexpectedly happy hunting ground for any would-be ghostbusters.

Harbour Oaks Inn

Address:	126 West Scenic Drive, Pass Christian, Mississippi 39571
Telephone:	(601) 452-9399
Facilities:	Smart bed-and-breakfast with lovely public rooms, nearby dining
Price Range:	Inexpensive to moderate

MONMOUTH PLANTATION

Natchez, Mississippi

Built around 1818 for General John Quitman, the Monmouth Plantation has earned the reputation as one of the most romantic places to stay in the entire United States.

Certainly, the general's grand plan for this lovely antebellum home was "to create an atmosphere of permanence and peace amidst a changeable world." He made that plan come alive as a wedding gift for his bride.

Present owners Ron and Lani Riches have preserved the general's dream in their careful restoration of this home, which had become dilapidated in recent decades. Since their acquisition of the property in 1977, it has become a luxurious home—a historic bed-and-breakfast reminiscent of the charming atmosphere of the Deep South.

There are nineteen guest rooms and suites, all furnished in period with carved bedsteads. There are comfortable sofas, antique clocks, and priceless objets d'art filling every corner. Some of the guest accommodations are in the main house, others in the restored Coach House, slave quarters, and other outbuildings set amid the nineteen-acre gardens.

Complimentary hors d'oeuvres are featured on the cocktail menu along with mint juleps. Dinners are five-course feasts, reputedly the best in Natchez. Regional specialties, using local produce, are served by candlelight. And the Christmas holiday season at Monmouth is right out of a fairy tale.

Natchez, once an important port on Ol' Man River, is now a town filled with boutiques, museums, and delightful mansions. There are atmospheric walks along the path down to Natchez-under-the-Hill (once the gambling center of the area), or along the levee. Baton Rouge is only a short drive away.

THE GHOST at the Monmouth Plantation is General John A. Quitman, hero of the Mexican War, and the original owner of the property.

When Ron and Lani Riches bought Monmouth Plantation in the mid-1970s, the house needed extensive restoration. Despite the sophisticated alarm systems installed to protect the property and the increasing number of valuable antiques within, there was often an intruder on the premises. The alarms were triggered, but no one—and nothing—could ever be found to account for them.

There would be heavy footsteps overhead, or in an adjoining room, when no one was there. And sometimes the footsteps seemed to carry the clink of spurs.

Construction workers, housekeepers, the Riches themselves—and even the police—have heard these unaccountable noises.

Research suggests they are caused by the spirit of General Quitman, who sadly did not live long in his new home. He took sick of a mysterious fever soon after moving in and languished for more than two years in his room upstairs before dying there.

Maybe the general just wanted to keep an eye on the renovations. Since they were completed, the footsteps and alarms have stopped. He seems to be pleased with his new quarters.

MONMOUTH PLANTATION

Address:	36 Melrose Avenue at the John A. Quitman Parkway, Natchez, Mississippi 39120
Telephone:	(601) 442-5852 or (800) 828-4531
Fax:	(601) 446 7782
Facilities:	Historic bed-and-breakfast, antiques, gardens
Price Range:	Expensive

CHICO HOT SPRINGS LODGE

Pray, Montana

THE STARS OF Montana shine bright over the century-old Chico Hot Springs Lodge. Stars of stage and screen come in droves to dine, dance, and even sing along at this renowned western hideaway. Nestling at the foot of Emigrant Peak, among low sage-covered hills, this inn is in real cowboy country.

The Yellowstone River runs right beside the property, a long, low, white-framed building where show-biz luminaries such as Jane Fonda, Jeff Bridges, and Dennis Quaid often come to "chill out." With all that national park wilderness on the doorstep, it's not surprising that guests at the lodge bring hearty appetites with them— promptly satisfied by produce from the Lodge's own spring-fed kitchen garden and dishes on the menu such as escargots "mountainique," crown of lamb, and mountain trout. The late Steve McQueen loved it here; he even rolled up his sleeves on occasion and helped with the cooking.

This old inn has guest accommodations in regular rooms, in chalets, log cabins, condos, or even motel units, all furnished in a rustic cowboy style, but with every modern comfort. There is a flourishing health spa with its own hot-spring pool, offering a range of fitness, health, and beauty regimes. And there is the Chico Saloon, jumping on Saturday nights, when musicians such as Warren Zevon and Jimmy Buffett sometimes drop in and play along.

The lodge is the focus for myriad outdoor activities in the area. Everything from hiking and riding to river-rafting and skiing is available within an hour or so's drive. The battlefields of the Indian wars are hereabouts, too, such as Little Big Horn, and there are a number of Native American settlements to visit, ghost towns and gold mines galore. The breathtaking scenery of Glacier and Yellowstone National Parks is on the doorstep.

THE GHOST at Chico Hot Springs Lodge is Percie, a real gal of the golden West.

Percie arrived in Chico from Canada in the late 1880s to seek her fortune. Despite there being few women in the territory at that time, and life being hard in general, Percie decided to make it her home.

Already in love with the sage-covered hills, she soon fell in love with pioneer Bill Knowles. Together they built the Hot Springs Resort, ran the accommodations at the lodge, and created the celebrated restaurant, health spa, and resort facilities.

All this took time. Before the resort achieved its deserved fame, it had taken its toll on Bill's health. He died in 1910, leaving the grieving and courageous Percie to keep the resort going through good times and bad. In the worst of the depression it proved too much for her. Percie "retired" to Room 349 where she spent her time rocking in her chair, enjoying the magnificent view of Emigrant Peak, and reading her Bible. She died in 1940.

Percie still keeps an eye on things. Regular reports have sightings of her slight figure all around the lodge. On one memorable occasion in 1986, she was seen floating above the piano in the lobby. Staff, security guards, and guests reported feelings of being watched when no one was nearby.

Percie's old room on the third floor still has her rocker. No matter how it is left in the room, it is always found facing the vista of the Absaroka Mountains and the commanding Emigrant Peak.

Percie's Bible was placed in the attic, away from meddling fingers. When staff have occasion to go up there, they check to see if it's safe. And they report the Bible is always found open, never a film of dust on its pages.

Another great character of Percie's time, and one fundamental to the success of the Chico Hot Springs resort's health facilities, was Doc Townsend, an old-fashioned country doctor recruited by Percie to put the spa and its treatment center on the map. He did just that in the early years of this century, while coping with everything from attacks of biliousness to brain surgery.

When Doc died, the lamp he kept burning in his office twenty-four hours a day went dark. It has defied every effort to relight it since then.

CHICO HOT SPRINGS LODGE

Address:	P.O. Drawer D, Pray, Montana 59065
Telephone:	(406) 333-4933 or (800) HOT-WADA
Fax:	(406) 333-4694
Facilities:	Hot springs, entertainments, sports
Price Range:	Inexpensive

GALLATIN GATEWAY INN

Gallatin Gateway, Montana

A RAILROAD COMPANY built the Gallatin Gateway Inn to be its "flagship" west of the Rocky Mountains. It opened in June 1927 with a "mammoth celebration and christening of this palatial structure." Although the hotel subsequently fell on hard times, it was saved to undergo a prolonged and accurate restoration. It re-opened in the late 1980s in all its former glory and is still worthy of its former flagship status.

The original carved beams are in place in the high ceilings; the tall, arched windows that are the trademark of the hotel reveal even more luxurious fittings than in days gone by; the checkerboard tile floor of the lobby gleams; parlor palms shiver in the breeze of the ceiling fans; and in the elegant dining room, the menu reflects regional and seasonal specialties.

The twenty-five guest rooms now include some suites and, like the building itself, are individual in character, furnished in comfortable western style, featuring folkweave fabrics and cowboy art.

The Inn was originally planned to be a summer resort for Yellowstone Park. But now it's a year-round destination in its own right, offering fishing (including its own casting pond), tennis, and pool with hot tub.

Both downhill and cross-country skiing at Bridger Bowl and Big Sky are only a half-hour drive away. Spanish Peaks and other wilderness areas are right on the doorstep for wildlife spotting, hiking, riding, hunting, and river-rafting.

THE GHOST at the Gallatin Gateway is Amelia, who worked at the inn one summer in the early 1930s.

Amelia was the seventeen-year-old daughter of a prominent family back East, who came to Montana to spend a summer working and "seeing life" just before going to college.

During that fateful summer, Amelia met and fell in love with someone her parents would regard as totally unsuitable—one of the groundsmen at the resort. She and her young man kept company for several months until the season came to an end. Then the staff dispersed to their homes, and the inn was closed for winter.

But Amelia became increasingly distressed at the thought of parting from her new love. At the last moment, she flatly refused to go home to Boston. Her parents' pleas were ignored. Letters were returned marked "gone away." Come that Thanksgiving, Amelia's family still had no news of her. By now thoroughly alarmed, her father took the westbound train to look for the young girl.

When he arrived at the deserted inn, Amelia's father set about rousing the caretaker. Once he had persuaded the man to unlock the property, they scoured every possible corner looking for traces of Amelia.

Downstairs, the rooms, corridors, and lockers held no clue of the girl's fate.

But upstairs, in a remote closet, the distraught father found the lifeless body of Amelia.

It has never been established whether the girl's death was an accident, the result of a broken heart, suicide, or murder.

Now Amelia's sad, restless, and forlorn spirit still wanders the north wing, and she is frequently seen by staff.

Her lover was never traced. But another sad, restless spirit, this time of a young man, is often seen roaming the inn's south wing. Separated in life, these young people are apparently still kept apart in death.

GALLATIN GATEWAY INN

Address:	P.O. Box 376, Gallatin Gateway, Montana 59730
Telephone:	(406) 763-4672
Facilities:	Tennis, fishing, skiing, riding, and hiking
Price Range:	Moderate

GARNET GHOST TOWN COTTAGES

Missoula, Montana

FOR A get-away-from-it-all vacation, stay in one of the cabins in the Garnet Ghost Town.

Back in the 1870s, Garnet was a real-life gold-rush boomtown—bustling, busy, and brash. Its name came from the semiprecious stones, a profitable by-product of the gold mines. Garnets can sometimes be found in the old spoil heaps, even today.

Like all boomtowns, Garnet was eventually hit by the inevitable slump. Gold fever moved on, the settlement declined, its population dwindled, and by the 1930s, the town had all but died. Now it has been brought to life by the Federal Bureau of Land Management and the Garnet Preservation Association. It has developed into a popular summer visitor destination. Its general store, saloon, and stables are as lively and as rowdy as they were in the town's heyday.

But in winter, the town goes back to sleep. There is the lovely scenery, the wildlife, the snow, and those hardy enough to rent one of the town's two refurbished guest cabins.

One, known as "The Newlyweds' Cottage," was built by Mr. Davies, the successful owner of the Garnet General Store. Whenever he heard of a young couple in the town hindered from marriage because they couldn't afford a place to live, he would loan them this shack free of charge.

[148]

Today the shack, and its neighbor, are far from spartan. While the buildings are original, their interiors are up-to-date: simply but very comfortably furnished with wood-burning stoves and rustic-style furniture.

Winter access is limited to snowmobile or cross-country skis. The nearest all-weather vehicular road is ten miles away. Bearmouth and Potomac are the nearest villages, while Missoula some twenty miles distant is the nearest big town.

THE GHOST of Garnet Ghost Town is the spirit of the old mining town itself.

Looking at the old clapboard settlement nowadays, it is hard to imagine it in its heyday around the turn of the century. Garnet was one of the most affluent gold-mining towns of the region, attracting sharp businessmen, tough miners, gaudy ladies, and earnest, hopeful settlers.

Today, Garnet sleeps through the deep Montana winters under a blanket of timeless snow. But in summer it springs to life, populated by characters from the good and bad old days. Desperadoes pop up at the saloon, covered wagons roll down Main Street, and gunfights erupt outside the Assay Office in a series of live, action-packed shows.

At the end of every day, when all the costumed characters and their props are accounted for, there is always a shadowy figure left on the sidewalk—a bewhiskered old-timer, a somber gunslinger, or a girl in a poke bonnet and homespun frock. The spirits stay on where they've always been.

Garnet Ghost Town may be dead, but it sure won't lie down.

GARNET GHOST TOWN COTTAGES

Address:	Off Hwy. 200, Box 8531, Missoula, Montana 59807
Telephone:	(406) 329-3914
Facilities:	Lots of open space
Price Range:	Inexpensive

MURRAY HOTEL

Livingston, Montana

THERE'S A GREAT party atmosphere at the Murray. Somehow this town-center property has a sparkle about it, whether or not there is any special function or holiday program in progress.

The hotel opened its doors in 1904, when it was known as the Elite Hotel, and immediately its ambiance attracted movie moguls, magnates, and madcap personalities of all kinds. Situated at one of the crossroads cities in Montana, the Murray was often "on the way" to and from the West Coast for characters as diverse as movie director Sam Peckinpah—who actually listed the Murray as one of his homes—and the late Queen of Denmark.

The Murray's galleried lounge has deep-buttoned leather sofas, masses of flowers, and some truly massive sets of antlers. The hotel's forty-three guest rooms are charmingly furnished with carved wooden bedsteads reminiscent of yesteryear and have every modern comfort. The renowned restaurant, the Winchester Cafe, is casually elegant. Its bill of fare includes award-winning dishes such as black bean cakes, scallops sautéed with ginger, and the vast Big Sky rib-eye steak. The lobby has an espresso bar serving delicious home-baked pastries, and there is even video gambling on the premises, a popular attraction for visitors and local residents alike.

Livingston is at the heart of Yellowstone country. World-class fishing, hiking, river-rafting, hunting, golf, and skiing are within an easy hour's drive of the hotel. And it is set among some of the nation's loveliest scenery.

Livingston itself has many delightful specialty shops and galleries, including the Parks Reece Gallery showing the work of that local artist.

THE GHOSTS at the Murray Hotel are two good-time girls from the early 1900s.

Often seen and heard around the hotel, they are both slight figures. One seen especially in Room 202 is wearing a glittering white evening dress. The other is only a faint wistful shadow on the fourth floor.

Both girls arrived at the Murray (then called the Elite Hotel) to enjoy some good times with Walter Hill, son of railroad magnate J. J. Hill. Walter Hill was smitten by the hotel on his first visit and retained a number of apartments in the old Elite on a long-term basis. He brought hordes of friends along with him to enjoy the grand balls and other frivolities for which the Elite was famous.

On one occasion, Hill was accompanied by humorist Will Rogers. So delighted were they with the warm welcome they received, they determined to share the experience with anyone and everyone. Full of high spirits and abundant bonhomie, the two madcaps added to the guest list a favorite saddle horse, which they took up to Rogers's suite on the third floor—via the 1905-vintage, hand-cranked Otis elevator!

It was impossible to keep track of Hill's guests, whether invited or gate-crashers. After one such shindig, the two good-time girls somehow stayed on.

The younger of the two, only around sixteen years of age at the time, fell madly in love with Hill, although he did not seem to care much for her. She followed him around like a puppy. He grew so weary of her clinging company that he virtually banished her to her rooms on the fourth floor and forgot about her.

One day, staff reported she was no longer there. Had she checked out? They couldn't say.

What happened to this dazzled little girl on the fourth floor, no one knows. But since then, staff and visitors staying in what were her rooms have experienced a number of strange phenomena.

Many people are aware of a presence, a feeling of not being alone, or they hear a girl giggling when no one is near. One housemaid, sleeping in what were the girl's rooms, woke to hear laughter, not of one young girl but of three—in tones that seemed slightly malevolent, as if planning a spiteful prank.

Another maid heard this laughter, then was startled to feel suffocated, as if a pillow had been pressed over her face. Collecting her wits, she told the gigglers to go away. They did, but only temporarily.

Was this young mistress of Hill's the victim of a practical joke that went wrong? Is that why she was not seen to leave? Is she still in her rooms on the fourth floor, teasing and being teased by Hill's other good-time girls?

Hotel owners Dan and Kathleen Kaul have heard the giggles. And once, telling a former owner proudly about the redecoration they had carried out on the fourth floor, they were startled to find the former proprietor becoming agitated, asking whether any of the walls had been stripped or replastered. When the Kauls asked why, the answer came, "If you plaster over the walls, she will not be able to come out."

Is there still a grim secret somewhere behind the light partition walls of the fourth floor? Could it be that this young girl was ousted by Hill in favor of the girl in the long white gown? Certainly, this second girl, one of Hill's long-standing amours, often stayed in the hotel in Room 202. Her slender, glittering ghost is often seen moving through what was her room, along the corridors, and down the stairs en route to the ballroom, on her way to a dance that ended almost ninety years ago.

Walter Hill certainly knew how to throw a party. Perhaps one ended in tragedy. Or perhaps these good-time girls had such a ball they cannot bear to return home.

MURRAY HOTEL

Address:	201 West Park, Livingston, Montana 59047
Telephone:	(406) 222-1350
Fax:	(406) 222-6547
Facilities:	Central location
Price Range:	Moderate

GOLD HILL HOTEL

Virginia City, Nevada

ORIGINALLY KNOWN AS the Vesey's Hotel, the Gold Hill Hotel is one of the few old buildings remaining in Virginia City's adjoining sister city, Gold Hill. Construction began in 1859, the same year a major gold deposit was found in Gold Canyon. Within a year, this region had become the world's wealthiest mining district.

The old stone part of the hotel is original and came complete with banqueting hall and saloon. But, when the gold rush faded, so did the hotel's fortunes. It became a miners' bunkhouse, then a private residence, before being restored and expanded into the luxurious country inn it is today.

The character of the old building remains. Inside the original stone walls, guests are transported back in time. All accommodations are decorated with period antiques, and the accommodations range from the four quaint rooms in the original building to the new "wing"— expansive suites equipped with fireplaces, wet bars, and balconies overlooking the Sierra Nevada Mountains.

The hotel lounge, the Great Room, is a popular meeting place and still attracts as varied a collection of characters as it did in the hotel's earliest days. Other public rooms include the patio and bar. The elegant Crown Point Restaurant is one of the highlights of the hotel and specializes in French cuisine and fine wines.

Theatrical performances—ranging from cowboy shows to Shakespeare—are staged at the hotel during the summer. Proprietor Doug

McQuide also arranges special events such as book signings, chamber music, and solo concerts throughout the year.

At an altitude of fifty-nine hundred feet, the hotel rests under brilliant blue skies and is surrounded by desert mountains. The area is perfect for hiking, biking, and exploring. Virginia City, with its shopping, Old West saloons, museums, mansions, and modern-day casinos, is right next door. During the summer, the towns are linked by the steam-powered trains on the Virginia and Truckee Railroad. Reno and Lake Tahoe are about forty-five minutes away.

THE GHOST at the Gold Hill Hotel is "Rosie." Nobody knows who she really was, but the hotel staff call her Rosie. Whenever she appears in one of the original bedrooms in the old part of the hotel, she is accompanied by the smell of roses. But Rosie is not alone. There is also a ghost named William, "the gentleman in Room 5," because that's where he likes to appear.

The 136-year-old Gold Hill Hotel, the oldest hotel in Nevada, is a link to the days of the Comstock Lode, the silver rush which came hard on the heels of California's gold rush. Miners and adventurers followed California's rivers back toward their source, panning for gold as they went in the hope of finding the lode of precious metal. They found one source in nearby Gold Canyon, but as they struggled to recover it, they cursed Gold Hill's sticky blue mud, which slowed them down and gummed up their machinery. Then they found the heavy blue mud was rich in silver.

So Gold Hill became a silver hill and turned Virginia City into a boomtown. And in 1859 the Gold Hill Hotel was built to cater to the miners and millionaires, prospectors and pimps, and gamblers and girls who flocked into town.

The old part of the building has been enlarged and modernized since then, but the old part remains, a two-story rectangle with four small bedrooms over the Great Room and the saloon.

That's where hotel maid Vickie Miller has seen Rosie, an old-fashioned-looking gal with long reddish hair, a white blouse, and a long skirt. Guests, too, have seen her. One even went down to the reception desk and complained there was a girl in his room.

"When he described her, we knew it was Rosie," Miller says.

Rosie might have been one of the hotel "girls" who in the early days were employed to entertain male guests. It is less easy to explain the presence of William in Room 5.

He, too, is dressed in the clothing of 150 years ago, with a Mormon-style hat. He is tall, thin, and always carrying a violin. But he has hit the wrong note with Miller, who blames him for hiding things. Her set of room keys, for example, disappeared completely.

Surely, a simpler explanation might be that she just put them down somewhere? Perhaps. After all, the keys did turn up eventually in the kitchen. They had been tucked neatly away—in the oven.

GOLD HILL HOTEL

Address:	P.O. Box 710, Virginia City, Nevada 89440
Telephone:	(702) 847-0111
Facilities:	First-class accommodation in quaint old surroundings
Price Range:	Inexpensive to moderate

LA POSADA DE SANTA FE

Santa Fe, New Mexico

THE STYLISH La Posada de Santa Fe is a very attractive hotel that crosses cultures. Adobe-style cottages contain the guest bedrooms, while the main facilities are contained within an old Victorian inn. The whole property is situated among six beautifully landscaped acres of gardens, right in the heart of downtown Santa Fe.

Wood-beam ceilings, hand-carved southwestern furniture, and paintings by local artists all testify to the hotel's authenticity. There are 119 traditional guest rooms and suites in all, and regular visitors suggest it is worth asking for one of the ninety rooms with their own Indian kiva-style (or beehive-shaped) fireplaces.

Because of the two contrasting styles of building, each room is different and could be described as reflecting some stage of Santa Fe's history. *Vigos*, *bancos*, and other elements of traditional adobe construction rub shoulders with the refinements of Victorian architecture. All rooms have private facilities and room service is available.

Dining is in the renowned Staab House Restaurant, which features Continental and New Mexican cuisine. The restaurant contrasts with the graceful Victorian bar and parlors, where visitors and the locals gather. Private dining is also available.

The grounds are lush with centuries-old pine trees, quaking aspen, and blossoming flowers—a wonderful setting for relaxation. Santa Fe lies close to the foothills at the southern tip of the Rocky Mountains, and the hotel's central situation puts the plaza—starting point for viewing the historic city center—and museums within easy walking distance. Outdoor sports (especially skiing), shopping, and visiting the many galleries are popular. There is a regular airport shuttle service.

THE GHOST at La Posada de Santa Fe is Julie—and while she may be a ghost, she is also one of Santa Fe's best-known and best-loved characters.

Julie was the wife of Abraham Staab, who in 1882 built the house which is now part of La Posada. Abraham Staab, a German immigrant, made his fortune as a major supply contractor for U.S. Army posts in the Southwest during the Civil War and became a highly respected citizen of Santa Fe. He returned to Germany to find a bride and came back married to the former Julie Schuster.

The couple moved into their beautiful brick house (it has since been stuccoed to look like adobe) in 1882, and Julie became one of the town's leading socialites, furnishing her house in smart eastern style and holding weekly afternoon teas "at home" in the yellow silk drawing room.

Behind the glitter, Julie led a troubled life. A conscientious mother, she was heartbroken when her baby son died after an illness lasting several weeks. Her hair turned white overnight. Determined to raise a large family, she had seven children in all. But there were medical complications, and eventually Julie died on May 14, 1896, at the age of fifty-two. Glowing obituary notices were mixed with a whiff of scandal, for Julie had not been seen at all during the final years of her life. It was said she'd gone crazy and had to be locked up. Certainly, she has shown no inclination to leave her former home.

"She's been wandering around for many years," said one former general manager of the hotel. People who have seen her have always described her as wearing "a dark flowing gown and a hood."

Julie is usually seen at the top of the grand staircase in the central building in the main complex of the inn. But she has also been spotted in the Nason Room, a small alcove off the main dining hall. These later appearances are interesting because the Nason Room is a relatively recent addition. In Julie's time this was a garden.

A former employee at La Posada, Alan Day, reported in 1979 that he was cleaning in the Nason Room late one night when the hotel was deserted and looked up to see a woman standing by the fireplace. She was wearing a long dark gown and was translucent, he said, "but I could see her dark eyes looking at me." With remarkable composure,

Day returned to his cleaning. When he looked up again, the figure had vanished.

Some locals, who say that sightings of Julie have fallen off in recent years, particularly since the hotel had her bedroom—Room 256—redecorated in its former Victorian style, believe she is still looking after her former home. One night, during a sudden cold snap, the boiler was lit and the heating turned on (a highly complicated procedure) without apparent human involvement. At that time, the boiler room key was missing.

Often Julie is just a "presence," noticed by employees and accompanied by a sudden and unexplained draft. But a security guard spotted her coming down the grand staircase one night when he was on his way up it. He turned and ran, and when he looked back, the figure had vanished. And during the Staab house's one hundredth birthday party in 1982, banquet captain Fred Palmer had a tray filled with champagne glasses tugged firmly out of his grasp by an unseen hand. "Just a playful gesture," he said afterward.

Since then, hotel telephone operator Gloria Valencia has found Julie, "beautifully dressed," sitting in an armchair early in the morning, quietly watching her work.

"I wasn't really frightened, just startled," Valencia says. When she looked back at the chair a few seconds later, the ghost had vanished. Another former employee to have seen Julie is Michael Corletti, who is now in a top tourism job.

Occasionally, guests in Room 256 sense Julie's presence and ask to be moved. But she is usually seen as a wispy figure on the stairs.

"I've no doubt she is here," said general manager Dottie Read. "There are too many people who've seen her."

LA POSADA DE SANTA FE

Address:	330 East Palace Avenue, Santa Fe, New Mexico 87501
Telephone:	(505) 986-0000
Fax:	(505) 982-6850
Facilities:	Adobe cottage-style rooms surrounding old Victorian inn
Price Range:	Moderate to expensive

ST. JAMES HOTEL

Cimarron, New Mexico

THE ST. JAMES HOTEL, now a national historic property, began as a saloon built in 1873 by the Frenchman Henri Lambert, who had been personal chef to Presidents Lincoln and Grant. At that time, Cimarron (it means "wild" or "unbroken" in Spanish) was a stop on the Santa Fe Trail, a really wild hangout for traders, mountain men, and desperadoes.

To begin with, the new hotel was a place of violence. Twenty-six men were killed within the two-foot-thick adobe walls. The notorious gunfighter Clay Allison is said to have danced on the bar, now part of an elegant dining room which still has bullet holes in the pressed tin ceiling.

But today the hotel is a place of quiet elegance, fine food and drink, expert and friendly service, and unsurpassed hospitality.

The St. James Hotel offers fifteen restored bedrooms, all beautifully decorated with antiques. Most have private facilities. These rooms are complemented by a modern twelve-bedroom annex, where all rooms have private bathrooms. The dining room is noted for its superb continental cuisine, and there is also a coffee shop, gift shop, and outdoor function area. The hotel stages occasional "Wild West Adventure" murder mystery weekends (price range: moderate).

Situated in the scenic foothills of the majestic Sangre de Cristo Mountains, the St. James Hotel is surrounded by excellent hunting and fishing areas, and is only minutes away from the Angel Fire and Red River ski resorts. Visitors can also enjoy the outdoor splendor of Valle Vidal Park and the Palisades in nearby Cimarron Canyon.

THE GHOSTS at the St. James Hotel are a trio of characters straight out of a western movie, which is hardly surprising when you consider this property was once a rough, tough, Wild West saloon. There is Mary Lambert, the wife of the hotel's builder, Henri Lambert, who still inhabits her old room on the second floor; gambler James Wright, who came to a sticky end right

ST. JAMES HOTEL

after winning a big poker hand; and a sort of poltergeist known simply as "the Imp."

James Wright is by far the most fascinating of the three. His presence was first noticed in Room 18 while the hotel was being refurbished in 1985. The reports were sufficiently convincing for the room to be shut and locked. It has been locked ever since.

Jacque Littlejohn, a psychic from Albuquerque, identified the mysterious presence as Wright. His winning poker hand earned him a huge prize, variously reported as an entire herd of cattle or even the hotel itself. But before he could collect his winnings, Wright was murdered. And, Littlejohn says, Wright's spirit is still waiting in the hotel to collect his winnings.

Fanciful stuff. Except that when the owners came to inspect the old hotel registers, they discovered a gambler called James Wright had indeed checked into the hotel just before the killing. His room number? Yes, you've guessed it: 18.

Meanwhile, Mary Lambert is still taking a friendly interest in the people who stay in the building her husband created. Guests frequently smell her perfume, and women brushing their hair sometimes get a helping hand from Mary, whom they feel touching their heads. Hotel historian David Kenneke has reported that both sensations are stronger if Mary likes the guests.

The aptly named Imp seems to confine himself to the kitchens and the bar, annoying staff by moving implements and bottles and, sometimes, causing these items to float through the air.

Owners Greg and Lori Champion, and Greg's brother Perry, have been working from old photographs to restore the hotel to the way it looked in the 1870s. Gunfights and gambling were common events in the saloon and the customers included Jesse James, Clay Allison, Wyatt Earp, Bob Ford, Buffalo Bill Cody, Bat Masterson, and Pancho Griego. This was not a bar to brawl in. Twenty-six recorded shootings took place in the saloon, with Clay Allison responsible for eleven of them. When a new ceiling was installed in 1902, more than four hundred bullet holes were found in the old one. No wonder the place is believed to be haunted.

But Greg Champion is anxious to point out that the ghosts for which the St. James is now famous do not haunt the hotel. They merely live there. And they add a whole lot of atmosphere to what once again looks like a very real chunk of the old Wild West.

ST. JAMES HOTEL

Address:	Route 1, Box 2, 17th & Collinson, Cimarron, New Mexico 87714
Telephone:	(505) 376-2664
Fax:	(505) 376-2623
Facilities:	Wild West hotel with peaceful ambiance
Price Range:	Inexpensive

BELHURST CASTLE

Geneva, New York

BELHURST CASTLE (the name *Belhurst* means "beautiful forest") is a turreted, red-stone building constructed in the latter half of the 1880s. Sitting atop a cliff among sweeping lawns and tree-shaded vistas, it overlooks Seneca Lake and combines the romance of the past with the comforts of the present in an elegant yet relaxed atmosphere.

The luxurious bedrooms and two-room suites—thirteen of them in all—are beautifully furnished, air conditioned, and have private facilities (although, in some cases, the bathrooms have only a shower). There is a TV set and telephone in every room.

A complimentary continental breakfast is offered all year, while Sunday brunch served in the dining room or on the terrace has become something of a local institution and includes free bloody marys and mimosas.

Unusual for a relatively small property, Belhurst Castle offers room service. Champagne in your room? Certainly, sir. Or if you prefer, you can draw yourself a glass of white wine from the spigot on the second-floor landing. But the restaurant is not to be missed. The wide-ranging lunch and dinner menus include price-fixed dinners and feature local wines.

Belhurst Castle also has its own banquet room, ideal for wedding receptions, gala holiday celebrations, or tour groups of up to three hundred people.

Belhurst Castle is centrally located in the middle of the Finger Lakes region, about one hour's drive from Rochester, Syracuse, and

Corning. Sonnenberg Gardens, Watkins Glen, the Finger Lakes wineries, and Hobart and William Smith Colleges are all within easy reach.

THE GHOST at Belhurst Castle is that of a beautiful Italian opera singer, who fled from Spain to America with her lover in the late eighteenth century and now seems reluctant to leave the gardens of what became her home.

The couple had good reason to flee Spain. Two men had fallen in love with the opera singer at the same time: a handsome young man and an older, married Spanish don. Within a few weeks, the handsome young man was dead from multiple stab wounds. The don was the chief murder suspect. Pursued by the authorities, as well as the don's humiliated wife and family, the opera singer and her murder-suspect lover escaped to America. There they joined up with a band of trappers and eventually arrived in the Finger Lakes region, where they set up home in a house that once stood on the site now occupied by Belhurst Castle.

The couple believed they would never be found there. But just in case, they had an emergency escape route, a secret tunnel running from the cellar of their house down to Seneca Lake.

For two years, the couple lived happily in their lakeside hideaway. Then one day their pursuers caught up with them, bent upon revenge for the humiliations they had suffered. The couple raced for their secret tunnel. Just as they were within sight of safety, the tunnel collapsed, killing both the opera singer and her pursuers.

The disconsolate don escaped. Broken-hearted, he spent the rest of his life in a monastery, grieving for his lost love.

All this is a well-known story locally but is almost certainly based more on fantasy than fact. No one can even be sure that the runaway coupled existed. And yet . . .

The secret tunnel would have run under what is now the castle lawn. Stories persist that it is still there. And, over the years, dozens of guests at the inn have reported seeing a woman in white standing silently on the front lawn in the middle of the night. Could it be the opera singer revisiting the spot where she died?

Another phenomenon sometimes reported by guests is the sound of someone singing to a baby during the night, even when there is no young mother or child staying at the inn. How this links up with the story of the romantic runaways is not clear. But a

BELHURST CASTLE

property such as Belhurst Castle ought to be surrounded by legends like this, for they complement the atmosphere of romance and add a touch of mystery.

BELHURST CASTLE

Address: Route 14 South, P.O. Box 609, Geneva, New York 14456
Telephone: (315) 781-0201
Facilities: Spacious rooms (including several suites), room service, restaurant
Price Range: Moderate

THE EDGE OF THYME

Candor, New York

IN THE CENTER of the Finger Lakes region, it's a matter of turning back the clock and spending time as you might have at the turn of the century when you stay at The Edge of Thyme bed-and-breakfast.

Nearly one hundred years ago, Rosa Murphy, private secretary to John D. Rockefeller, met Dr. Amos Canfield in New York City. They married and decided to spend their summers in Candor, where they created a Georgian home in the center of the village. Rosa's elegant style became well known.

The well-maintained formal home exists now much as it did then, with its leaded glass-windowed porch, marble fireplaces, parquet floors, beautiful stairway, gardens, pergola, and gracious atmosphere.

There are just four guest rooms, two of them with private baths. Hosts Professor and Mrs. Frank Musgrave say that "well-behaved children are always enjoyed." This, coupled with a nearby kennel for pets, makes The Edge of Thyme suitable for family holidays. Smoking is not permitted. A full breakfast is served, in a style befitting a turn-of-the-century property, and afternoon tea is also available by appointment. There is on-the-spot antique shopping.

Candor is close to the southern tip of Cayuga Lake, and it is only a short drive to Cornell University and Ithaca College. A trip out to Watkins Glen, Corning, Elmira's Mark Twain country, Binghamton, and Cooperstown can be enjoyable, as well as visits to the many wonderful wineries in the region and the New York state parks.

THE GHOSTS at The Edge of Thyme are probably a former Civil War soldier and his wife, who once lived there. The old soldier can still be heard walking around the house, while a woman believed to be his wife has been seen in a rocking chair in one of the guest bedrooms.

The inn's charming and hospitable owners did not like the idea of buying a haunted house. When they purchased it, they specifically

THE EDGE OF THYME

asked whether the property had a ghost. They were told it did not, and in 1984 they moved in.

"After a few weeks my husband and I realized we had heard footsteps but thought it might be someone walking by," Eva Mae Musgrave recalls.

One evening they were both in the former ballroom when they heard someone with leather-soled shoes walk down the stairs and through the house from one end to the other. No problem about that, except the stairs were heavily carpeted. Also, whoever had walked through the house had also walked through two locked doors.

"We continue to hear footsteps at various times, either day or night," Mrs. Musgrave says.

Indeed, their basset hound, Winston, is so attuned to the phenomenon that he now ignores the footsteps. Mrs. Musgrave says she also hears the sound of women talking, "as if they are playing a game or having tea," when there is no one there.

"We never mention having ghosts, because not everyone is amused," Mrs. Musgrave says.

That makes it all the more extraordinary that two quite different guests, on different occasions, have reported waking in the night and finding a blonde woman in a long white dress sitting in the rocking chair next to their bed. The Musgraves also noticed one window in the house, which they kept locked, continually opened by itself—always during the day.

A psychic who made an unplanned visit to the inn, and who apparently knew nothing of its history, offered a possible explanation. She told the Musgraves that the Civil War soldier and his wife remained in the house because the wife was buried beneath the basement and her husband refused to leave. The old soldier was, she added, "very uncomfortable" because the house had been remodeled. The wraparound porch with steps on which he had taken the air had been removed. It was he who opened the locked window, again to get some air.

Not surprisingly, the Musgraves were skeptical. But the house had been remodeled in 1908, so they dug out an old picture and found that it used to have, yes, a wraparound porch. What's more, the mysteriously opening window was right where the porch steps had been. At that point, Mrs. Musgrave felt she had nothing to lose. She asked the old soldier if he would mind not opening the window on winter days, but she wouldn't mind if he continued to open it on dry summer days.

"For nearly two years the window never opened," she says. "Last summer, on nice days, it opened several times."

Women guests have also had perfume bottles removed. Although they don't mind their unseen guests, the Musgraves have never made a point of advertising these stories.

"I enjoy my guests, both alive and spiritual," Mrs. Musgrave says. "So do my husband and Winston. Winston raises his head and cocks his ears but no longer bothers to bark at noises, footsteps, or voices. Fortunately, the brave basset is a lot more welcoming towards tangible visitors. He recognizes nice guests."

THE EDGE OF THYME

Address:	6 Main Street, Candor, New York 13743
Telephone:	(607) 659-5155
Facilities:	Stylish bed-and-breakfast, afternoon teas
Price Range:	Inexpensive

RUFUS TANNER HOUSE

Pine City, New York

THIS 1864 VICTORIANIZED Greek revival farmhouse bed-and-breakfast holds a commanding position on a small knoll surrounded by century-old sugar maples still tapped to produce maple syrup each March.

While the house retains its Victorian charm, it has been comfortably updated. There are always flowers in bloom, indoor and out, while dwarf fruit trees make up a small but peaceful orchard in which to sit or stroll.

There are three double-bed guest rooms on the second floor, all with private bath. They are tastefully but simply decorated and have period furniture. The master bedroom, on the first floor, is particularly memorable, with marble-topped high-Victorian furniture, a pine floor, period wallpaper, and a European-style bath with two-person shower and whirlpool tub.

Big rooms and antique furniture abound. The kitchen has an ornate cooking stove, and the wainscoted dining room (where guests are served breakfast of their own choosing) has a Victorian fireplace and period furniture. Guests can also use the living room, with its baby grand piano, and the flower-filled TV room. There is even a sort of minigymnasium in the basement, with a weight machine and treadmill. A newly installed outdoor hot tub is proving popular. Smoking is not allowed anywhere.

Attractions in the Elmira-Corning region include Elmira College, various sites connected with Mark Twain, the Arnot Art Museum, and the Corning Glass Museum. And, of course, the beautiful Finger Lakes are only just to the north.

THE GHOST at the Rufus Tanner House is the spirit of a man who hanged himself in a nearby barn that has since been pulled down. There is an overgrown cemetery across the field behind the Rufus Tanner House, the suicide's last resting place. Except that his spirit isn't resting.

"The first time I saw this spirit I was fifteen years old and sleeping out on the porch with a friend," innkeeper William Knapp says. "I awoke in the middle of the night, seemingly for no reason, and started looking around the yard. About 120 feet away was an old milkhouse and next to it was what appeared to be a man all in white. I watched on and off for [what seemed like] an eternity. I blinked, rubbed my eyes, squinted, held them shut for several minutes. I did everything I could to be certain it was not my vision. Finally, when I looked out after a brief time, it was gone."

It was five years before Knapp was to see the ghost again. One summer's evening, just before dark, he and a couple of young ladies who were sisters were amusing themselves in the kitchen. The younger sister got tired of the others teasing her and decided to go home. She got about halfway from the house to the old barn when she ran back screaming. All three of them went out and, says Knapp, "There, to our surprise, was the same specter I had seen many years before. We all saw it—and I had never mentioned the previous incident to anyone."

Faced with a figure from the spirit world, the teenage trio proved remarkably spirited themselves. They didn't run: They threw stones at it. Knapp's stone passed right through the ghostly white figure and hit the barn door, then the figure faded away.

Since then, Knapp reports other strange occurrences, "too many to mention." But he recalls in particular a tenant in an apartment over the kitchen whose table lamp started turning itself on and off one night. Fearing an electrical fault, the tenant went to unplug the lamp and found himself stepping into a cold spot, despite the fact that the room was draft-free.

In 1933, a young couple staying in one of the inn's bedrooms reported seeing a ghost in their room during the night. They said, "It was just standing there, and then it disappeared." That would seem to bear out a story told to Knapp by a very old lady, born in the Rufus Tanner House in 1900. She said there was a ghost there, and her entire family had felt its presence many times.

"It had never bothered any of them any more than it bothers us," Knapp says. "It never creates any disturbance. It just seems to be there, possibly observing what's going on.

"There is no predictable time or place to see the ghost. It's just around."

RUFUS TANNER HOUSE

Address: 1016 Sagetown Road, Pine City, New York 14871-9137
Telephone: (607) 732-0213
Facilities: Private baths throughout, basement minigymnasium
Price Range: Inexpensive; ask about weekend and honeymoon
packages

SUTHERLAND HOUSE

Canandaigua, New York

BUILT IN 1885 by farmer and banker Henry C. Sutherland, this Victorian house has been completely renovated and restored by innkeepers Cor and Diane Van Der Woude, and is now run as a Victorian-style bed-and-breakfast.

The rooms are all beautifully appointed and have private baths. Two of the rooms, the Parkerhouse Suite and the Dutch Treat Suite, feature two-person whirlpool baths and have TV sets and VCRs. All the rooms have double beds, and a smoking ban operates (except outside).

Restoring the house was a labor of love for Dutch-born Cor Van Der Woude. A carpenter who works in the maintenance department at Rochester University, Van Der Woude says, "I like remodeling. I've learned to treat it as a hobby rather than making it a chore."

Although things like the plumbing, heating, and windows had to be replaced, the Van Der Woudes have been able to retain such original features as the marble fireplaces and a winding cherry wood staircase. This has helped to make the house, which is also the Van Der Woudes' home, exceptionally atmospheric as well as warm and welcoming. Visitors with special diets are catered to, as long as the Van Der Woudes are notified in advance.

With Rochester only a half-hour away, and the Finger Lakes close by, Sutherland House is superbly situated. Local attractions include antique shops galore, boating and lake excursions, breathtaking fall foliage, skiing on Bristol Mountain, plenty of golf, music, and winery tours. Rochester stages its Lilac Festival in May, and places especially worth visiting are the Cumming Nature Center, the Granger Homestead and Carriage Museum, and the Sonnenberg Gardens and Mansion.

THE GHOST at the Sutherland House is hopefully little more than a memory now, but the Victorian-Gothic property—which bears more than a passing resemblance to the Bates residence in *Psycho*—had a bad reputation in Canandaigua for years.

When Van Der Woude and his wife, Diane, bought the house in 1993, they found it water-damaged, full of trash, and overrun by raccoons.

"It looked forlorn and desolate," Diane Van Der Woude recalls. "It looked like it needed a hug."

But when they started digging into the house's history, the couple found it had something of a reputation, too. "When we met people, we would tell them about our house and they'd say, 'Oh, the haunted house,' or 'the witch house' or 'the Munster house,' " Diane Van Der Woude continues.

Worried, the Van Der Woudes checked with the previous owner, an artist who had not helped the house's reputation by keeping a life-size doll in the yard.

"But she said the only spirits here were kind spirits," Diane Van Der Woude says.

Since then, she and her husband have changed the house's pale gray color, which gave it "the appearance of being possessed," and have extensively renovated, restored, and decorated it inside and out.

"We've never had the feeling of ghosts at all," Diane Van Der Woude says. "That was just the reputation the house had.

"We were truly drawn to this house. A peaceful feeling came over as we entered. We have hugged the house, and the house has hugged us back."

SUTHERLAND HOUSE

Address:	5285 Bristol Street, Canandaigua, New York 14424
Telephone:	(716) 396-0375 or (800) 396-0375
Facilities:	Four rooms all with private bath, special diets by arrangement
Price Range:	Inexpensive

10,000 DELIGHTS

Branchport, New York

DESCRIBING ITSELF AS "a bed-and-breakfast that transcends the ordinary," 10,000 Delights certainly has a name that transcends the ordinary. It was chosen by innkeeper Vera Van Atta who, after reading of an ancient Buddhist tradition which maintained the world is made up of ten thousand things, realized that her own world was composed of ten thousand delights.

One of those delights was discovering the old inn during a winter ride with her husband, Bruce. Standing in a fairy-tale setting of gullies, woods, and waterfalls, with Lake Keuka as a backdrop, the battered building was derelict—inhabited only by a family of raccoons. But the couple fell in love with it, bought it, and spent their spare time restoring it. And, although Bruce sadly did not live to see the work completed, 10,000 Delights opened its doors to guests in July 1989.

An 1850 Greek revival mansion overlooking the lake, the house is filled with antiques and original works of art, and features eight themed guest rooms. Victoria's Room contains an 1852 watercolor of the old queen; the Lavender and Lace Room is as romantic as its name suggests; the Medieval Room boasts a velvet-draped four-poster feather bed, and so on.

The rooms in the main house share bathrooms, although if you are desperate, Vera Van Atta promises "the prettiest three-seat outdoor privy on the lake." The only accommodation with a private bath is the three-bedroom beach house, although there is also a honeymoon apartment with its own whirlpool bath.

Additional outbuildings include a studio-cum-herb shop and a picturesque stable beloved by artists. The Japanese Teahouse is perched on top of a sixty-foot waterfall, which flows under the glass-panelled floor. 10,000 Delights has its own lakeside beach, with boating for guests, and Branchport's famous Saturday market is a favorite excursion.

10,000 DELIGHTS

THE GHOST at 10,000 Delights is the property's former owner, Bertha Jane Von Kamecke, who innkeeper Vera Van Atta believes "called" her to restore the old property. There is also a ghost named "Rose," who haunts the Yellow Rose Room. "And charming ladies they are," Van Atta emphasizes.

She blames artist Bertha Jane for continually putting her own pictures in prominent positions when the Van Attas were restoring the house.

"I would totally clean a room, and when I returned the next day, there would be one of Bertha Jane's framed pictures on the wall, or an unframed watercolor behind the door," Van Atta recalls.

She continues: "A few years ago, I mentioned to a guest that Bertha Jane must have moved on, because I no longer 'felt' her around. The next morning I went up to the Victorian Bath and found the heavy antique beveled mirror, usually hanging over the sink, lying in the middle of the floor, face up and not broken. The hook was still in the wall, and the mirror had to crash over a marble sink before it landed.

"I went into the adjoining Blue Lounge and there, in the middle of the floor, was the long antique mirror whose regular position was on the wall above the couch. Again it was face up, unbroken. It would have had to jump six feet over the coffee table to land in that spot.

"At that point, I thanked Bertha Jane for alerting me to the fact that she was still in residence and watching over us!"

Rose, on the other hand, remains quietly in "her" Yellow Rose Room. Nobody seems to know who she is or what she is doing in the house, but one thing is certain—she doesn't like the bedroom door closed. That can be an inconvenience for guests, so, when the door-opening got to be a menace, Van Atta fitted a hook-and-eye latch on the inside of the door. That fooled Rose for a few months, but then she learned how to open that, too.

"Rose is very fond of bits and pieces in 'her' room," Van Atta continues. "Last summer a guest played the mechanical music box as she unpacked. When it ran down, she forgot it. But in the middle of the night, the music box started playing again and continued until she got up and thrust it into a suitcase."

10,000 Delights might have a third ghost. One night, a guest staying in the Medieval Room was awakened by the smell of baking and found a mysterious man standing by his bed. "I like my scones with raisins," the specter said before quickly vanishing. And even that may not complete the family of phantoms. A psychic has told Van Atta, "There are lots of spirits here. They love the place!"

10,000 DELIGHTS

Address:	1170 West Lake Road, Branchport, New York 14418
Telephone:	(607) 868-3731
Facilities:	Attractively situated bed-and-breakfast, lots of Victoriana
Price Range:	Inexpensive

THENDARA INN

Canandaigua, New York

THENDARA IS A Mohawk Indian word meaning "the meeting place," or "fork in the road," and is the name chosen by Senator John Raines for the lavish, cottage-style retirement home he planned and built for himself on a forty-five-acre bluff beside Canandaigua Lake at the turn of the century.

The property, four miles out of Rochester, was later used as a club-house by the Canandaigua Yacht Club. In 1975 it became a restaurant; present owners Rick and Joy Schwartz then took over in 1987 and undertook a major restoration and modernization of the building to create a warm and graceful five-bedroom inn.

Each guest room has its own bathroom, TV, and ceiling fan, while the suite also features a skylit Jacuzzi. The property is air conditioned and furnished with turn-of-the-century antiques to match its architectural style.

The Thendara Restaurant, which occupies the same building, is famous statewide for its uncompromising excellence.

THE GHOST at Thendara Inn is Senator John Raines, who built the house as his retirement home in the early part of this century. He did not live to enjoy the property of which he was so proud.

Operations manager William Bonetti, who has worked at the inn for eight years, says, "I have had many encounters with the senator." In particular, he reports numerous phantom telephone calls from Room 2 when there is nobody staying there.

Guests claim to have heard footsteps and banging doors during the night, and the inn's staff tend to blame the senator for any mechanical or electrical faults. Some of these manifestations are rather strange, such as the time Bonetti's desk top drawers all slid gently open of their own accord while he was sitting at the desk.

But only one person can actually claim to have met the ghost, a waitress named Michelle. As she and Bonetti were leaving the inn one

THENDARA INN

evening recently, Michelle remembered she had left her purse in the kitchen and went back to fetch it. As she opened the kitchen door, Bonetti heard her say, "Bill, is that you?" He called out that he was waiting by the front door. But in the half light provided by a single lamp over the stove, Michelle had seen and felt a dim figure brush lightly past her before disappearing.

The senator has played some other tricks, including meddling with the lights in the restaurant's Longview Room. It's just as though he is making himself at home in the house he meant to retire to.

THENDARA INN

Address:	4356 East Lake Road, Canandaigua, New York 14424
Telephone:	(716) 394–4868 or (716) 398-2780
Fax:	(716) 396-0840
Facilities:	Property includes well-known Thendara Restaurant, with additional coffee shop boathouse restaurant on lakeshore in summer
Price Range:	Inexpensive

LODGE ON LAKE LURE

Lake Lure, North Carolina

THE LODGE on Lake Lure is, as its name suggests, right on the lakeshore. It is the only lakeside inn in Hickory Nut Gorge, one of the most scenic areas in western North Carolina. Nestled among the foothills of the Blue Ridge Mountains, the lodge is across the lake from Rumbling Bald Mountain and just far enough from the center of town to be secluded. The views are breathtaking.

The lodge is a large, rambling structure at the end of a wooded drive. The main lounge—the Greatroom—is warm and inviting with vaulted ceilings, hand-hewn beams, panel walls, and a twenty-foot stone fireplace with a huge gristmill stone embedded in the chimney. Through the french doors lies the breakfast room, which is really a sun porch with lots of glass for enjoying the scenery. A separate reading room is furnished with books, games, TV, and videos.

Downstairs, the rocking chairs are all lined up on the Lakeview veranda. A terraced walkway meanders down to the boathouse and deck, a popular spot for sun-seekers and lake-watchers as well as boatmen.

There are eleven guest rooms, all individually styled and comfortably equipped. They all have private bathrooms. The home-baked breakfasts vary from day to day and feature family recipes. Although other meals are not served at the inn, there are plenty of good restaurants throughout Hickory Nut Gorge.

This inn is for relaxing, rather than a touring base. Days out of doors and evenings around the fire are its attraction. If your pleasures are a jug of wine, an intimate yet private environment, fine art and antiques standing side by side with family photos, and innkeepers in jeans who love to swap stories, then this is the place to stay.

THE GHOST at the Lodge on Lake Lure is George Penn, a highway patrolman shot and killed by two criminals in 1937. The lodge was built in his memory as a retreat for state troopers and their families. It was not until much later that it became a bed-and-breakfast. Present innkeepers Jack and Robin Stanier took it over in 1990.

"Our ghost is not a headless horseman," Robin Stanier laughs. "Just a nice, mild-mannered fellow, who most of the time is just there."

The Staniers didn't know they had an uninvited guest until a woman who was staying in Room 4 told them, "There's a ghost in my room." The guest had awakened in the night to find a man walking around the room and, thinking he had made a mistake, she called to him, "Wrong room." He then walked out into the hallway. The guest woke her husband to tell him what had happened, and he sleepily pointed out the bedroom door was closed and locked.

A few weeks later, Robin Stanier told another guest this story but didn't mention the room number. The guest said excitedly that the same thing had happened to her. A check revealed that she, too, was staying in Room 4.

Intrigued, the Staniers called the inn's previous owner, who admitted there was a ghost. Naturally, this became a topic for animated conversation during the Stanier family's Christmas lunch at the inn. Adult daughter Betsy, expressing disbelief, said, "If there is a ghost, I wish he'd do something." He did. A large glass goblet standing at the back of the buffet table flew across the room and shattered.

People who don't want to admit in front of other guests they have seen a ghost often take Robin Stanier aside to tell her of their experiences with the phantom cop.

"No one seems unduly upset or even seems to feel any fear," Stanier says. "Every single witness has been the same kind of person—very calm."

In fact, George's only "victim" has been a little girl who was staying at the inn with her mother. When a potted plant flew across the room in front of the harassed mother, she immediately assumed that her daughter was responsible and gave her a real dressing-down. But according to Stanier's daughter, who witnessed this incident, the little girl had been nowhere near the potted plant before it became airborne.

But if George Penn really is around, there could be no spookier setting for a ghost than Hickory Nut Gorge. The region is full of legends. The Cherokee Indians avoided it because they said it was the home of "little people" and spirits. Tales of the "little people"—a bit like European fairies or leprechauns—still abound in the valley.

There are also stories of a ghostly cavalry battle being reenacted in the sky during the nineteenth century, and "a crowd of specters" seen floating up toward Chimney Rock at about the same time. As the afternoon shadows lengthen in the valley, the atmosphere can certainly seem very strange. It is possible to believe almost anything.

People say, for example, there is buried treasure on Round Top Mountain. But perhaps oddest of all, there are signs in the gorge of a very early, pre-Indian civilization which lived there and knew how to mine gold and smelt iron. Who were they? Not even the archaeologists know—and the evidence is so flimsy they probably never will.

LODGE ON LAKE LURE

Address:	Route 1, Box 529A, Lake Lure, North Carolina 28746
Telephone:	(704) 625-2789 or (800) 733-2785
Facilities:	Spectacular and peaceful setting, own boathouse
Price Range:	Inexpensive to moderate

REXMONT INN

Rexmont, Pennsylvania

THIS ELEGANT VICTORIAN mansion near Rexmont was built in 1875 for the elegantly named Cyrus Rex, a wealthy nineteenth-century banker and store owner. A small, intense-looking bachelor, Rex lived in the house with his niece, Susan Amanda. The pair were popular in the locality because Rex often helped the townsfolk buy their own homes by arranging mortgages. His own home deteriorated after his death, and it was not until a couple of years ago that Janet Ruby and her husband, George, began converting it into an upscale inn.

Now, the bedrooms are immaculate, with elegant furnishings, family antiques, and private baths. Breakfast (including champagne breakfasts) comes served on antique china. English afternoon teas served by the grand fireplace in the drawing room are a feature of the inn. They will even arrange for a butler to attend you, if you wish.

After their first experience with ghosts, the Rubys called in a psychic, and, as a result, a whole series of special psychic weekends (price range: moderate) are now a feature of the inn's annual program. Other special themed holidays include health and beauty spa therapy weekends; theater packages; romantic weekends; birdwatching breaks; and even a weekend linked to the Herschey Antique Auto Show held locally.

Less formal entertainments and interests include special lectures in the inn's extensive herb garden and performances of chamber music in the library. For main meals, there is a good restaurant opposite the inn.

Local attractions are the Cornwall Furnace Museum, only a mile from the inn, Mount Gretna, and the Middle Creek Waterfowl Area.

The Herschey complex is about sixteen miles away; Gettysburg is a little over an hour's drive. Horseback riding is available very close to the inn.

THE GHOST at the Rexmont Inn is Susan Amanda, the niece of the house's builder, Cyrus Rex. She lived there first with her uncle, then with her two daughters, until her death in 1924.

Innkeeper Janet Ruby says, "Susan comes into the bedroom that bears her name, the Susan Amanda Room, and sits on the bed. It has happened twice in the last couple of years, to guests who did not know about our ghost story."

There have been spooks around ever since George and Janet Ruby bought the old house in 1992. Workmen who were renovating the building complained they were being "watched" by a figure standing behind them, who disappeared when they turned around. Janet Ruby, a skeptic at the time, laughed it off. Then, the night before the inn opened, it happened to her.

"I was standing in the Cyrus Rex Room and I felt it, too," she says. "When I turned around, no one was there."

She later saw a "shimmering" figure in the second-floor hallway, where there used to be a tower. Her father, who was living in the inn at the time, heard what he described as the rustle of a woman's gown behind him and felt an invisible presence brush past. They both heard footsteps and banging doors upstairs when the inn was empty and experienced lights turning on and off. Even George Ruby, still a skeptic, admits that clocks behave erratically.

Two couples have given detailed and remarkably similar reports of feeling someone sitting down on the bed in the locked Susan Amanda Room during the night, and of seeing "a form" rise and stand at the foot of the bed. Neither couple knew about the ghost, and neither felt that the apparition was at all threatening.

A reporter for *Mid-Atlantic Monthly* magazine who spent a night in the Susan Amanda Room saw nothing, but she did detect a heavy and overpoweringly sweet floral smell at one spot in the main hall. Janet Ruby's sister has also said that there is sometimes "the smell of funeral flowers" in the same spot. There is no explanation for this.

Of her own experiences, Janet Ruby says, "They didn't frighten me." But she feels that the figure she "felt" in the Cyrus Rex Room, and saw in the second-floor hall, might have been Cyrus himself.

It is well known that Rex and his niece were very happy during the twenty-seven years they spent together at the house. So it would be nice to think that they are both still there. Perhaps the series of psychic weekends at the inn will reveal more.

REXMONT INN

Address:	299 Rexmont Road, Box 127, Rexmont, Pennsylvania 17085
Telephone:	(717) 274-2669, or for reservations and information (800) 626-0942
Facilities:	Upscale activities including afternoon tea, special psychic weekends
Price Range:	Inexpensive to moderate

BULLOCK HOTEL

Deadwood, South Dakota

A GENUINE PIECE of the old Wild West in historic Deadwood, the Bullock Hotel must have come as a bit of a relief to the townspeople when Sheriff Seth Bullock built it over the remains of his burned-down hardware store in 1895. Until then, gentlemen could find a bed only in one of the local bordellos or flophouses—ladies had nowhere to stay at all.

Complete with a turkish bath, a reading parlor, and big brass beds in its sixty-three rooms, the original Bullock Hotel was considered one of the finest hostelries in the West. And it still is. Meticulously restored to its former grandeur, it offers new Victorian furnishings, big beds, hospitality bars, and, in some suites, Jacuzzi tubs (price range: moderate).

But some things never change. Gaming still goes on around the clock in the high-ceilinged ballroom, just as it has for almost one hundred years, although the slot machines have added a flashy new look and there are no wild-eyed gunslingers cheating at the blackjack tables.

Bully's Restaurant and Lounge serves thick cuts of steak and fresh seafood beside a crackling fire, and the meals are complemented by fine wines and imported beers. Seth's Cellar, deep below the hotel, opens its doors for special occasions such as top musical and variety acts, melodramas, historic vaudeville shows, dinner shows, and films depicting the history of the Black Hills. Guests at the hotel enjoy off-street parking, and there is an in-house gift shop.

The hotel is situated in the heart of Deadwood, which has been recreated as an old lead mining town. There are dozens of historic

BULLOCK HOTEL

gaming halls all along Main Street and countless museums and other attractions. Mount Rushmore, Wind Cave, Badlands National Park, Devils Tower, and Spearfish Canyon (of *Dances with Wolves* fame) are all only a short drive away.

 THE GHOST at the Bullock Hotel is "Old Seth" Bullock, the first sheriff of Deadwood and a character straight out of the Wild West. His friends included Wild Bill Hickok and Calamity Jane, although he didn't think much of either of them.

[184]

Bullock's life story reads like a film plot. Born in Ontario, Canada, in 1849 to a Scottish mother, he quickly clashed with his army officer father's strict code of discipline and left home to "go West, young man." A politician at twenty, and a founder of Yellowstone National Park at twenty-three, he was a sheriff in Montana by the time he was twenty-four. When he joined the gold rush to South Dakota in 1876, he was a natural choice as one of the leaders of the lawless community that sprang up around Deadwood Gulch. He was appointed town sheriff in 1876 after the death of Bill Hickok, masterminded the rebuilding of what is now the Bullock Hotel, became a rancher, fought as a captain in the Spanish-American War, and befriended a man named Teddy Roosevelt. When Roosevelt became president, he appointed Bullock a U.S. marshal. Upon Roosevelt's death in January 1919, Bullock erected a monument to him in the famous Black Hills of Dakota on the crest of the newly renamed Mount Roosevelt. Bullock died later the same year.

That might have been the end of the story but for two very strange postscripts. First, in 1991, the owners of the Bullock Hotel got a letter from British psychic medium Sandy Bullock, saying that a spirit named Seth Bullock was trying to make contact and was giving the name of Deadwood in America. Could he be a relative, he wondered? And secondly, during reconstruction work on the Bullock Hotel in 1993, resident proprietor Mary Schmit, her employees, and several workmen all experienced a series of strange phenomena.

Schmit and her aunt, who lived with her at the hotel during reconstruction work, often heard their names being called when there was no one there. A massive new bar with a twelve-foot plate-glass mirror, in the lobby awaiting installation, fell over with a crash that shook the building—but without breaking the mirror. At the back of the lower floor, which seems to be the most haunted part of the hotel, employees heard footsteps when there was no one around. Two reported seeing a tall shadowy figure in cowboy dress. Schmit's sister, Susan, was alone in the building when she heard the pots and pans being clattered in the kitchen, and promptly locked herself in the cellar for the night. There, according to Mary Schmit, Susan "smoked an entire pack of cigarettes—and she doesn't even smoke."

The British Bullock, Sandy, said he was getting his messages through a Sioux named Singing Water. He might indeed be related to Old Seth. He has nothing to gain financially from either his "family" connection or his revelations, and, oddest of all, he has answered ambiguous test questions, submitted by American experts, quite correctly. But for a man who has never been to America, he does seem to have something of a fixation with the characters more easily found in western films than western folklore.

"Calamity Jane was just a whore, and Wild Bill Hickok murdered more people than those accused of the same crime," Seth Bullock said in one alleged message via Sandy Bullock. The same message went on to suggest that Wild Bill would have been better named "Back Shoot Hickok."

"Back Shoot Hickok"? That's fightin' talk. Things could soon get a lot wilder in this corner of the old Wild West.

BULLOCK HOTEL

Address:	633 Historic Main Street, Deadwood, South Dakota 57732
Telephone:	(605) 578-1745 or (800) 336-1876
Facilities:	In-house gaming
Price Range:	Inexpensive

NEWBURY HOUSE

Rugby, Tennessee

WELL OVER one hundred years ago, the settlers who founded Rugby enjoyed comfortable lodging at this charming, mansard-roof boarding house. And guests can still stay there today, for Historic Rugby, the company which now runs the old town, has restored Newbury House and opened it to overnight guests.

Each of the five bedrooms is furnished with Victorian antiques, some of them from the original town itself. There is a parlor for guests, and relaxing on the front veranda is a favorite pastime. Tea and coffee are available, free of charge, at all times.

There are no other catering facilities at the house, however, so breakfast is served each morning at the historic, wood-beamed Harrow Road Cafe. This is a full Cumberland Plateau home-cooked meal.

Historic Rugby is a touch of Victorian England in the Tennessee Cumberlands. More than one hundred years ago, its British founder described it as "a lovely corner of God's earth." Now, the National Trust calls it one of the "most authentically preserved historic villages in America." Even more colorfully, and fitting for a settlement intended to be a utopia, one writer described it recently as "Utopia in the wilderness."

Listed in the *National Register of Historic Places* since 1972, Rugby stands in a rugged river gorge setting where more than twenty of its decorative, gabled buildings remain. Christ Church Episcopal (where the 1849 organ is still played for Sunday services), the Thomas Hughes Library with its collection of seven thousand Victorian volumes, the

NEWBURY HOUSE

Kingstone Lisle cottage, and the Schoolhouse Visitor Center are all open daily for tours except in January.

THE GHOST at Newbury House is an Englishman named Mr. Oldfield, who in the 1880s was sent out from London to report on the progress of what was then a fledgling British colony.

"He liked the place so well, he sent to England for his son and wife to join him. But he died of heart failure at Newbury the night before his son arrived," says Barbara Stagg, executive director of Historic Rugby, Inc., the preservation trust which now runs the old town.

Rugby was founded in 1880 by Thomas Hughes, the English social reformer and author of *Tom Brown's School Days*. Hughes envisioned a utopian community atop the beautiful Cumberland Plateau of East Tennessee. He planned an attractive little town, full of lawns, ornamental gardens, and gravel walkways, overlooking the gorge of the Clear Fork. The town, which Hughes named after the school in his book, had to be hewn out of the wilderness. By 1884, about 450 latter-day British colonists had moved in. Some local Americans, mostly skilled craftsmen and farming families, were invited to join the community which was run on Christian Socialist lines. There was a single interdenominational church. For all Hughes's forward-looking philosophy, however, the town, which he called "the new Jerusalem," quickly became an upper-class, English-style settlement with a very Victorian atmosphere. Everything stopped for afternoon tea, and everyone dressed for dinner.

But drought, fires, an outbreak of typhoid, and the place's sheer inaccessibility took their toll. Many of the settlers soon moved on. Hughes died in 1896, having lost thirty-five thousand dollars of his own money on the project. It was not until the 1960s that attempts began to preserve what was left of the town.

Since then, both restorers and the new residents are aware that the town's former residents still seem to be in occupation. The town is one of the most haunted in America and proud of it. "At the Halloween Ghostly Gathering each October, we share our 'spirited' history with visitors, calling up the spirits of our dear departed 'Rugbeians,'" Barbara Stagg says.

That should be a spine-chilling occasion at Newbury House, where several guests have reported waking in the night to find the ghostly figure of a man bending over the bed—particularly in Rooms 2 and 4.

It might be Mr. Oldfield, looking for his beloved son. But there is another possible explanation, because when Rugby was built it had a hostelry called the Tabard Inn, named for the inn in Chaucer's *Canterbury Tales*. Utopia or no, the manager of the Tabard Inn murdered his wife in Room 13 by cutting her throat, then poisoned and shot himself.

A few years later, the Tabard Inn was destroyed in a fire. But the colonists were able to save some of the contents of the inn, including much of the furniture from the fateful Room 13. Some of the furniture found a new home in Newbury House, where it remains to this day. And who knows what spirits might have moved with it?

NEWBURY HOUSE

Address:	Historic Rugby, P.O. Box 8, Rugby, Tennessee 37733
Telephone:	(615) 628-2441 or (615) 628-2269
Facilities:	At the heart of a preserved historic village
Price Range:	Inexpensive

HOTEL OVERALL

Wartrace, Tennessee

KNOWN UNTIL RECENTLY as the Walking Horse Hotel, this property was closed and awaiting renovation at the time of this writing. It will reopen as the Hotel Overall, its original name from the late nineteenth century when it was built by Jesse and Nora Overall. The theme of the remodeled hotel is to be transportation, with the emphasis on railroads and horses.

The Hotel Overall, which is in the *National Register of Historic Places*, has played a part in the development of both forms of transportation. Wartrace was a major railroad town in the 1930s. The tracks still run close to the hotel. Also in the 1930s, when Middle Tennessee was becoming known as "the walking horse capital of the world," Wartrace was home to perhaps the most famous example of that high-steppin' breed, the gentle giant "Strolling Jim."

Strolling Jim, who in 1939 became the first world grand champion, was stabled behind what was then the Walking Horse Hotel. The grounds of the hotel have become Strolling Jim's final resting place; his grave is a place of homage for Tennessee walking horse enthusiasts.

The man who trained Strolling Jim to world championship standard in only five months was Floyd Carothers, who owned both the hotel and the stables. His wife, Olive, who operated the hotel from 1933 to 1958, was an avid collector of Tennessee walking horse memorabilia. This historic collection has been on display at the Walking Horse Hotel and will continue to be shown in the Hotel Overall.

A large, cool, echoing building, the new-look hotel will doubtless wish to continue its predecessor's reputation as a haven for Tennessee home cooking, featuring family recipes served at large tables in the spacious front hall.

THE GHOST at the Hotel Overall is Floyd Carothers, the hotel's former owner and the man who trained Strolling Jim. Until recently, the hotel was owned by George Wright, whose grandfather was Floyd Carothers's business partner. Wright kept

HOTEL OVERALL

up the hotel's most famous tradition by becoming an enthusiastic trainer and breeder of Tennessee walking horses. The stables at the rear of the hotel were Wright's pride and joy.

In Carothers's day, the horses were guarded by a large and very fierce watchdog. But George Wright went one better. According to him, the entire property has an even more frightening guard—the ghost of Floyd Carothers.

Fearsome Floyd is still something of a family figure around the hotel. When I first met Wright in 1991 and he told me his story, I was inclined to scoff. Without comment, he produced a picture taken in the hotel dining room in the early 1980s and originally intended for use in the hotel brochure. It showed him and a guest, Edwina Chilton, seated at a table in the dining room—with two indistinct, slightly glowing figures standing behind the chairs. Another photograph, taken of an empty table set for four, shows a quartet of the apparitions, one behind each chair.

The photographs were taken by the aptly named Ed Camera, of New Bedford, Massachusetts, who was adamant there had been no trickery. Says Wright, "These photographs confirmed our conviction that the hotel is occupied by spiritual entities."

He has much more proof. The protective Floyd persistently interfered with the hotel's security cameras, and in 1991, he pestered Wright nonstop when the hotelier was busy. Eventually, Wright succumbed to the spectral pressure and went across to the stables. He found his prize walking horse mare, who was about to foal, having difficulties.

Professional help was called in and at 1:30 A.M. on July 2, 1991, Lucky Chance was born.

"Many complications surrounded the birth and without the notice, Chance would not have made it," Wright said, when he wrote to tell me his happy news.

Oddly enough, Olive Carothers, the late Floyd's wife, passed away at about the same time. Floyd's activities abruptly ceased.

"Shortly after her death, I noticed the hotel had lost its spiritual relationship with Floyd," Wright says. "It appears he left the hotel. There have been no ghostly sightings since Ms. Olive died."

Or have there? Back in 1991, when he first showed me the photograph of the ghosts, Wright also showed me some family photographs, taken in the hotel's dining room by a different photographer, with a different camera, at a different time.

There was a tragedy in Wright's family some years ago when his brother, serving in the U.S. Navy, was killed on active service in the Far East. Since then, when the family gathers at the hotel to celebrate Thanksgiving or Christmas, they sit at a long table set up in the big entrance hall/dining room. On such occasions, they have traditionally left an empty chair for Wright's much-loved and still-mourned brother.

One recent Christmas they decided to take a family portrait of everyone seated at the long table. But when the picture was developed, there was a surprise in store. Seated in the empty chair, there was a clear outline of a man in naval uniform.

Not surprisingly, Wright is unwilling to discuss his family's loss any further, let alone part with the picture. But I have seen it. And I have little doubt that there are spirits—albeit quite modern ones—who still inhabit the Walking Horse Hotel as it undergoes metamorphosis back into the Hotel Overall.

HOTEL OVERALL

Address:	P.O. Box 266, Wartrace, Tennessee 37183
Telephone:	(615) 389-6407
Facilities:	Restaurant specializing in Tennessee home cooking, adjacent Tennessee walking horse stables
Price Range:	Inexpensive

GREEN MOUNTAIN INN

Stowe, Vermont

BUILT AS A private residence in 1833, the Green Mountain Inn became a gracious hotel in the mid-1800s. Tastefully restored for its 150th anniversary, the inn today offers a warm blend of modern comforts and authentic country charm.

Each of the sixty-four guest rooms and suites has its own special character. Many have queen-size canopy beds, fireplaces, and Jacuzzis. Stenciling, draperies of early American design, and country quilts all help to create an atmosphere of old-fashioned ease.

Dining is in one of the inn's two acclaimed restaurants. The famous Whip Bar and Grill, named for its collection of buggy whips, is casual. Main Street Dining Room is a gracious colonial dining room where guests can enjoy all meals, including a hearty Vermont country breakfast.

Guests enjoy complimentary use of the inn's fully equipped health club and heated outdoor swimming pool. The Stowe Recreation Path offers strolling, jogging, and biking among beautiful mountain vistas. In the heart of Stowe Village, the inn is surrounded by restaurants, boutiques, and antique shops.

In winter, Stowe is justifiably known as "the ski capital of the East," with forty-five superb alpine trails on Mount Mansfield, Vermont's highest peak, and 150 kilometers of groomed trails for cross-country skiing enthusiasts. No wonder the Von Trapp family, of *The Sound of Music* fame, settled here: It must have felt just like home.

THE GHOST at Green Mountain Inn is Boots Berry, a tap dancer and local hero who can still be heard dancing on the third floor of the hotel during severe winter storms.

Boots Berry's connection with the Green Mountain Inn in general, and with Room 302 in particular, was extraordinary. The son of the inn's horseman and a chambermaid, he was born in Room 302 in 1840. At that time the third floor of the hotel was the servants' quarters, and the boy grew up in and around the building. When he was in his twenties, he succeeded to his father's job.

Boots was a respected horseman. One of his duties was to provide fresh horses for the daily stagecoach. So he was on the spot in the main street of Stowe one summer's morning when the team bolted. Boots bravely stopped the runaway stage, saved the lives of the passengers, and was awarded a hero's medal. News of his exploit spread and, in the words of a local newspaper report, "Boots's popularity was such that there wasn't a place in the county where he could pay for his own drinks."

That was to be his downfall. Boots turned to a life of wine, women, and song, neglected his duties at the inn, and eventually had to be dismissed. He then wandered the country, picking up his nickname when he was jailed in New Orleans and learned to tap dance from a fellow prisoner.

Eventually, at the beginning of 1902, Boots drifted back to Stowe, shabby and poverty-stricken. At about the same time, a dreadful storm hit the town and a little girl somehow got stranded in the snow on the roof of the inn. But Boots, remembering his own childhood days, knew of a secret route to the spot where the child was, climbed up to her, and lowered her safely to the ground.

Just as the girl reached safety, Boots slipped and fell to his death from the icy roof. His life had come full circle, for the roof he was standing on when he fell was the roof of Room 302.

If the sound of tap dancing on stormy days is anything to go by, he is still around. One member of staff even claims to have met him in the corridor. Marketing director Darcy Walsh believes that Boots is a spirit to be proud of, and adds, "Most of us here believe there really is a ghost at the inn."

GREEN MOUNTAIN INN

Address:	P.O. Box 60, Main Street, Stowe, Vermont 05672
Telephone:	(802) 253-7301 or (800) 445-6629
Fax:	(802) 253-5096
Facilities:	Excellent accommodations in town known as "the ski capital of the East"
Price Range:	Moderate

MAPLEWOOD INN

Fair Haven, Vermont

THIS LOVINGLY RESTORED Greek revival-style home, dating back to around 1843, is listed in the *Vermont State Register of Historic Places*. Formerly the residence for an old dairy and creamery called Maplewood Farm, the house was left empty when the dairy buildings were torn down in 1981. But in 1986, work began to transform the old house into the Maplewood Inn and Antiques.

Today it is a warm and inviting inn, in the heart of central Vermont's lake region. A relaxing and romantic property, Maplewood Inn has comfortable bedrooms and a big choice of public rooms, all full of antiques. There are panoramic views from the house and wonderful sunsets from the porch.

There are five lovely bedrooms, decorated in period style: the Patio Room, the Oak Suite, the Rose Room, the Blue Room, and the Hospitality Suite. The Rose Room and Hospitality Suite can be joined to form a two-bedroom suite. All the rooms have private baths, cable TV, and air conditioning. Most have roomy seating areas with a fireplace. In-room telephones with private numbers and photocopying are available on request, to make the property attractive for small business meetings.

Public rooms include the Keeping Room, with its fireplace. The Gathering Room houses the library; and the parlor has a complimentary cordial bar. If you prefer stronger drinks, there is a tavern area, but it is operated on a bring-your-own basis. Room rates include a buffet breakfast, which is largely continental in style and includes home-baked products.

There are good shops and restaurants nearby. Local attractions include the Vermont State Fair (in September); Lakes Bomoseen, St. Catherine, and Champlain; skiing at Killington, Pico, and Okemo; Wilson Castle; Chaffee Art Center; and a selection of activities ranging from riding and golf to attending plays or picking apples. Fair Haven is equidistant from the airports at Albany, New York; Burlington, Vermont; and Lebanon, New Hampshire.

THE GHOSTS at Maplewood Inn are a young couple with a little girl, a strange white figure who seems to emerge from an old trunk, and an invisible cigar smoker. All of these have been experienced by guests at the inn, who have provided detailed accounts of what they saw.

Take, for example, Lillian Simcox, of Oradell, New Jersey. She was in the bedroom known as the Hospitality Suite between 11:00 and 11:30 P.M. on the night of February 13, 1993, taking part in a Scripture-reading group with seven other women.

She states, "Most of the women had their eyes closed. I happened to have my eyes open and suddenly a young couple with a little girl walked from the bedroom entrance into the living room of the suite where we were all seated. They walked through the living room, then down the stairs as if they were headed for the first floor.

"It was extremely vivid. The man was wearing a black suit and carrying a carpet bag. The woman was wearing a long blue dress with a shawl and was carrying her hat in one hand and holding her little girl's hand with the other. They were dressed in 1800s dresses. I was not frightened. In fact, it was a comforting feeling. One of the other women, Barbara Tietjen, also saw the couple."

Needless to say, no such family was staying in the inn at that time. Simcox also smelled cigar smoke in the Gathering Room next morning, an oddity in a no-smoking property; and a similar phenomenon is reported by innkeeper Cindy Baird. Baird has also heard the sound of someone playing ball when her husband, Doug, was asleep and there was no one else in the house.

Back to the guests' experiences, which the Bairds have carefully recorded and retained. Kathy Jackson of Powell, Ohio, reports she was staying in the Oak Suite with her husband on September 24, 1994, when she awoke between 2:00 and 3:00 A.M. and went to the bathroom. When she got back into bed, she saw, rising from the old trunk at the foot of the bed, "a man-sized-and-shaped white form. It was not very clear, but I could see eyes and the vague shape of a man about six feet tall."

The startled Jackson tried to awaken her husband, but he "simply rolled over." So she closed her eyes and thought "this can't really be happening."

She concludes, "I did not look again and assumed he had left. I was not really afraid and told many of my friends about the incident."

Earlier, Jackson had tried to open the trunk because she wanted to find an extra blanket, but the lid would not budge. The Bairds are puzzled by this, because the old trunk has no lock. They say it contained only old, nineteenth-century clothing and that it was found in the suite before it was converted from an attic.

Cindy Baird adds, "The bedroom of this suite is located directly over our living quarters and on several occasions we've heard loud bangs, as if something fell or someone had jumped on the floor upstairs. We always went up to check and never found anything out of order."

This wing of the house was once an old tavern across the street, which was pulled down and rebuilt as part of the Maplewood Inn. Cindy Baird says, "Several times, while working at my desk in our quarters, with the door to the parlor open, I could have sworn someone was walking in the hall, since the boards squeak. I looked, but no one was there."

Curiouser and curiouser. One suspects there are a lot more strange stories to emerge from the Maplewood Inn.

MAPLEWOOD INN

Address:	Route 22A South, Fair Haven, Vermont 05743
Telephone:	(802) 265-8039, or for reservations (800) 253-7729
Fax:	(802) 265-9210
Facilities:	Top-class property, antiques, some office services
Price Range:	Inexpensive to moderate

LINDEN HOUSE

Champlain, Virginia

LINDEN HOUSE is a restored planter's home, built around 1750 in a rural setting and now run as a charming bed-and-breakfast. The house is in the *National Register of Historic Places.*

There are six bedrooms—the Robert E. Lee Room, the Jefferson Davis Room, the Essex Room, the Linden Room, the Coachman Room, and the Footman Room. Spacious and comfortable, these rooms all have double beds and are stylishly furnished with antiques. Bathrooms are either private or semiprivate, while two of the rooms share a Jacuzzi and steam bath.

In addition to these rooms, the ground-floor level of the old Coach House has been converted into the self-contained Carriage Suite (price range: moderate), which has country-style and antique furnishings and its own fireplace. Many of the rooms overlook the English garden. All told, there are more than two hundred acres of landscaped grounds to admire and plenty of quiet places to sit outside and enjoy the peaceful setting. Children under twelve, pets, and smoking indoors are all discouraged by hosts Kenneth and Sandra Pounsberry.

A full plantation breakfast is served every morning, and coffee and lemonade are "on tap" all day. Linden House also accepts dinner reservations for parties of ten people or more.

Although Linden House enjoys a rural setting, it is only minutes away from historic Tappahannock, Stratford Hall, Wakefield, and other attractions. River cruises are available on the Rappahannock River, and there is plenty of good golf nearby. Tappahannock and the

LINDEN HOUSE

surrounding area boast plenty of fine restaurants and endless opportunities for antique shopping. But many guests seem content with one of the five porches at Linden House, a rocking chair, and a good book, for this is a place to relax in the old-fashioned way.

THE GHOST at Linden House is an unidentified shadow who drifts around in the hallway outside the Robert E. Lee Room, and a strange light seen inside the room itself.

While they were restoring Linden House, which had stood empty for thirty years, Ken and Sandra Pounsberry and their daughter often slept in the Robert E. Lee Room, jamming the bedroom door shut with a piece of wood (the lock didn't work) and leaving the light on in the hallway outside.

"Sandra and I noticed on different occasions that the light, which could be seen through the keyhole, would disappear at times as though there was some obstruction on the other side," Ken Pounsberry says.

They blocked the keyhole with paper but then noticed the same phenomenon reflected in the strip of light over the door. Was someone, or something, wandering silently up and down the hallway outside?

The Pounsberrys were commuting from their other home and business in Maryland at the time and in July 1990 left building contractor Matthew Hipple alone at Linden House. One night, Hipple was sitting and reading his newspaper when his hat "jumped off the back of a chair and across the room." Nothing too strange about that, perhaps, except an unseen hand then tried to open a bag of candy on the arm of the chair. Hipple, a believer in ghosts, refused to stay in the house again.

As a result, a week later, Pounsberry found himself back in the Robert E. Lee Room again and all alone. The annoying light was back on the ceiling and Pounsberry recalls, "It suddenly changed to an unusual form, moving slightly and taking on a flesh-like color. This was very frightening. I was hoping that it was a dream—but it wasn't."

When Ken Pounsberry told his wife what had happened, she admitted she had experienced a similar phenomenon in the same room when he wasn't there.

"It was alarming, but we tried not to let it disturb us and our work," Pounsberry says. "We relied heavily on our faith and as time went on we knew something was there but never let it frighten us."

As far as they know, the light has not returned since. But they have often heard unidentified footsteps in the house and voices that sound like "something on the recorder of an answering machine."

The problem with having phenomena like these, rather than a good, "solid," identifiable ghost, is what do you tell the guests?

"We try to give only slight details, or avoid commenting altogether," Ken Pounsberry says. "We have noticed that if we acknowledge what exists here, then more disturbances occur."

On the other hand, the Pounsberrys were happy for Linden House to be included in this book. Ken Pounsberry said, "I hope this will enlighten people to the fact that ghosts exist. Perhaps one day we will understand why these spirits are still here."

LINDEN HOUSE

Address:	P.O. Box 23, Tidewater Trail (Route 17), Champlain, Virginia 22438
Telephone:	(804) 443-1170 or (800) 622-1202
Facilities:	Antique furniture and setting, plantation-style breakfasts, some dinners by arrangement
Price Range:	Inexpensive

MARTHA WASHINGTON INN

Abingdon, Virginia

SET DEEP IN the quiet Virginia countryside, in the charming town of Abingdon some three hundred miles from Richmond, is a beautiful mansion built in 1830 for General Francis Preston. It is now the wonderfully atmospheric Martha Washington Inn.

Having survived the ravages of the Civil War and almost one hundred years as a girls' school, the former Preston house could almost do duty as a living museum. Many of its original features are preserved, enhanced by period furnishings and antiques, and a degree of comfort and service that recalls the gentler lifestyle of our forefathers.

At "Martha's," as this historic home is affectionately known, the sixty-one guest rooms offer the highest degree of modern comfort. Your bed might well be the house's original four-poster or half-tester bed. The silverware at dinner in the main restaurant, the First Lady's Table, is of the period, too, and the menu reflects the southern cuisine of the house in its pre-Civil War heyday. Highlights include quail, mountain trout, and Martha's Hot Fudge Cake.

There is an English-style pub bar, filled with memorabilia of the "late unpleasantness," and the main dining room boasts a hand-beaten tin ceiling. There is a wonderfully ornate art deco dining table sixteen feet long that had been "lost" in the rambling cellars below the house. It is almost impossible to avoid superlatives—the garden lawns are immaculate, with camellias and magnolias. Also, there is a gazebo. Complimentary afternoon tea is served on the wide front porch, and Martha's home-baked cakes are to die for!

Abingdon is a delightfully Victorian town, its shops featuring fashions, antiques, and fine arts and crafts. The famous Barter Theater has a full seasonal program. There are beautiful national parks nearby around Mount Rogers, and the Appalachian Trail passes close. The Virginia Creeper Trail originates in Abingdon and follows a historic and scenic route to the foot of White Mountain.

THE GHOST at the Martha Washington Inn is Beth, a student at Martha Washington College during the Civil War.

The inn had become a girls' school just before the Civil War broke out. As hostilities became increasingly violent, the house was turned into a hospital, with college staff and students doing their best to nurse the wounded of both sides.

One day, a Yankee officer, Captain John Stoves, was among the seriously wounded brought to the school. Consigned to a room on the third floor and to the care of Beth, a girl with staunch Confederate sympathies, Stoves was too severely wounded to survive. Despite Beth's tender care and her prolonged attempts to keep him alive, Stoves's strength waned.

As the end drew near, Stoves called for Beth, an accomplished violinist who often cheered the wounded with lilting songs and bright tunes.

"Play me something, Beth. I'm going," Stoves whispered. And, for the last time, Beth played the soft, beguiling southern melody that had comforted him so often.

After Stoves died, the weeping Beth, weakened by watching at his bedside through so many long nights, took to her bed. A few days later she, too, died—some say of the typhoid so prevalent at the time; others say of a broken heart. The Yankee soldier and his Rebel nurse now lie side by side in Abingdon's Green Springs Cemetery.

Whatever the cause of her death, Beth's playing of soft southern songs on her violin can still be heard echoing faintly through the rooms on the third floor of the Martha Washington Inn, especially on nights when the moon floats full over the mountains.

Beth's spirit is not lonely at the inn, for there are two other ghosts known to frequent it.

One is the ghost of a young Confederate soldier who was in love with an Abingdon girl during the troubled time when the town was caught between Confederate forces to the west and Union troops to the east.

Entrusted with a dispatch for General Lee describing the Union forces' position and strength, the young soldier broke his journey at Martha Washington College to bid his sweetheart good-bye. Creeping up the stairs, he was surprised by a reconnoitering party of Yankees, who fired on him.

The rash youngster fell at his sweetheart's feet in a pool of blood. And his blood stained the floorboards so deeply that the marks are still there. Every effort to remove them has succeeded only temporarily. Today they are covered with carpet, in what is now known as the Governor's Suite.

Love of a different kind has given the Martha Washington Inn its third ghost.

On a moonless night in December 1864, Abingdon fell victim to its first invasion by Union troops. The Yankees were few in number and were routed by Confederate forces. But one Union soldier escaped on horseback along the alley east of the school before being felled by a chance shot. The wounded soldier was carried into the college, where he died just as the clocks of the town struck midnight.

The Yankee's horse would not leave its master. The animal followed him on to the school's grounds and restlessly paced the lawns waiting for him to come and ride. At midnight, as his master died, the horse silently left the college gardens and was never seen again.

Well, almost never. For sometimes, on a dark and moonless night, a ghostly riderless horse is seen waiting on the south lawn.

Martha Washington Inn

Address:	150 West Main Street, Abingdon, Virginia 24210
Telephone:	(703) 628-3161 or (800) 533-1014
Facilities:	Dancing nightly
Price Range:	Expensive

PFISTER HOTEL

Milwaukee, Wisconsin

WHEN THE DOORS of the Pfister Hotel first opened on May 1, 1893, it was acclaimed as the ultimate in elegance and style. That elegance is still represented by the hotel's showpiece: its fine collection of nineteenth-century Victorian works of art. More than eighty original oil and watercolor paintings are permanently on show in the grand hallways and public rooms. It probably is the largest collection of its kind in a hotel anywhere.

But the age of elegance is not only on show in the paintings; it also continues to be represented by the hotel itself. A recent restoration has combined this historic grandeur with modern amenities so that guests of long ago, such as President McKinley or even Buffalo Bill, would still recognize their surroundings even if they didn't quite understand what to do with items such as VCRs and fax machines.

The 307 guest rooms and suites are all beautifully furnished and decorated, and the bathrooms are stunning. The Tower rooms offer a spectacular view of Milwaukee's celebrated lakefront, while the suites have a variety of amenities ranging from personal sitting rooms to Jacuzzis.

The lobby area in particular has been beautifully restored. It now contains the spacious lobby bar and lounge, overlooked by a dramatic ceiling mural of a clear sky-blue scene of heavenly cherubs, reminiscent of the lobby's original skylight.

For a midday meal or the regal Sunday champagne brunch, the Cafe Rouge is a Milwaukee tradition. Other restaurants are the Cafe at the Pfister, which is a European-style bistro, and the award-winning English Room—the hotel's dining showplace.

After one hundred years, the original "Grand Hotel of the West" is still just that.

THE GHOST at the Pfister Hotel is an old man who most people think must be Charles Pfister, the founder of the hotel. Certainly, Pfister was very proud of the hotel, so it's only to be expected that he's still keeping an eye on things.

"No one seems to know who first spotted him, or when," concierge Peter Mortenson says. "But he has been reported on the landing of the Grand Staircase, surveying the lobby. Another time he was seen in the minstrel's gallery above the Imperial Ballroom, and yet another time up on the ninth floor in a storage area."

The sightings have always been late at night and have always been the same: a portly, elderly gentleman, well dressed and with a cheerful smile. And when the witnesses have been shown a picture of Charles Pfister—who completed the hotel building project started by his businessman father, Guido Pfister, in 1893, and named the property after him—they have always uttered cries of amazement and exclaimed, "That's him!"

At least, that's what people say. Finding someone who has actually seen the ghost, or identified him from his picture, is harder.

"These stories have been told around here for years, handed down, like so much of the tradition of this grand hotel, from one generation of Pfister employees to the next," Mortenson says. "How much stock to put in them is anyone's guess."

PFISTER HOTEL

Address:	424 East Wisconsin Avenue, Milwaukee, Wisconsin 53202
Telephone:	(414) 273-8222 or (800) 558-8222
Fax:	(414) 273-8082
Facilities:	Superb collection of Victorian art in regal setting
Price Range:	Expensive

FERRIS MANSION

Rawlins, Wyoming

THE FERRIS MANSION is a classic Queen Anne-style Victorian home. The three-story brick house is a Barber pattern book design and was placed in the *National Register of Historic Places* in 1982.

Julia Ferris built the mansion in 1903, after her husband, George, had been killed by a runaway team of horses as he returned from his copper mine in the Sierra Madre. Julia lived in the mansion until her death in 1931 at the age of seventy-six. Later, the property was converted into apartments. Work on the restoration of the house started in 1979. The bed-and-breakfast began in 1986 with a single bedroom; today the Ferris Mansion has four, run by its owner, Jamie Lubbers.

The whole house offers a step back in history to the romantic elegance of days past. A grand oak stairway leads up to the second-floor bedrooms, all of which are spacious and quiet with authentic Victorian decor. Two have a fireplace; all four have private bathrooms and a TV set. An additional room, the Maid's Room, is available for a third person traveling with a couple, or for one or two well-behaved children. That bathroom is shared.

The downstairs parlors and a reception room with a grand piano are open to guests, and the large porch (with swing) is popular. Breakfast is buffet-style and consists of granola, assorted homemade breads and caramel rolls, juice, and fresh fruit. Pets are not allowed: They would upset the resident cat.

Rawlins is an old ranching and mining town and, at sixty-seven hundred feet above sea level, there can be a nip in the air. Tours of the

FERRIS MANSION

Old Frontier Prison, half a block away from the Ferris Mansion, are available on request. Saratoga is twenty miles away; Laramie, one hundred miles; and Yellowstone Park and Salt Lake City, about three hundred miles.

THE GHOST at the Ferris Mansion is Cecil, one of the seven children born to Julia Ferris. He is heard on the second and third floors of the house when no one is around, and in the hallway.

Julia Ferris was no stranger to tragedy. Besides losing her husband in the accident described earlier, four of her children suffered premature deaths. Cecil was particularly unfortunate. He was accidentally shot by one of his brothers when he was nine years old. An older brother had brought a pistol into the house and left it on a table in his bedroom. Some of the younger boys found the gun and, not knowing it was loaded, started playing with it. Cecil was shot through the neck as he walked through the doorway and died instantly.

But the boys are still up to their tricks! The footsteps heard on the second and third floors sometimes sound adult and are attributed by some to George Ferris. But there can be little doubt that the running footsteps in the hallway and the slamming doors are ghostly games of the sort that small boys play.

And, like all small boys, Cecil particularly likes annoying little girls. One young guest, preparing to clean her teeth, watched in amazement as her toothpaste came flying off the counter. Other guests have caught a half-glimpse of a ghostly figure on the open stairway and in the dining room.

But the oddest experience reported by a guest was when she noticed a woman watering the flowers outside the house very early one morning, only to find that none of the women of the house had arisen early that morning. Could Julia Ferris be back at the Ferris Mansion, keeping a maternal eye on her mischievous family?

FERRIS MANSION

Address:	607 West Maple, Rawlins, Wyoming 82301
Telephone:	(307) 324-3961
Facilities:	Victorian-style bed-and-breakfast accommodations
Price Range:	Inexpensive

OLDE ANGEL INN

Niagara-on-the-Lake, Ontario

To STEP THROUGH the doors of this, one of Ontario's oldest inns, is to step back into history. Looking remarkably like an English pub, the inn has lots of exposed hand-hewn beams and thick plank floors. The latter sometimes still seem to echo to the sounds of the British soldiers and townsfolk who have gathered here for food and drink for two centuries.

Small but unique, the inn is believed to have been founded around 1789, when it was called the Harmonious Coach House. At that time, Niagara-on-the-Lake was called Newark, and was destined to become the first capital of Upper Canada. Newark was the first place in the world to abolish slavery. Legislators celebrated the passing of their innovative new law with dinner at the inn.

All the guest bedrooms are furnished in simple colonial style. Besides a wealth of beams, they feature four-poster canopy beds. But modern additions mean they also have private bathrooms and color TV. Because the inn is so popular, advance reservations are advised. Room rates (particularly inexpensive in winter) do not include breakfast, but this is available on request.

The restaurant offers fine dining at reasonable prices. The nerve center of the inn is the English Pub, running across the front of the building and popular with residents and locals alike. The pub has a wide selection of ales and draft beers and also serves a variety of hearty snacks. A relatively recent addition is the Shaw Wine Bar, featuring fine Niagara wines.

Niagara-on-the-Lake has its own summer Shaw Theater festival. It is a charming little town, full of tempting craft shops and good restaurants. Niagara Falls is only a short drive away, and because you are on the Canadian side of the border, you'll see the vast Horseshoe Falls close up. Especially recommended: the boat trip to the foot of the falls on the *Maid of the Mist.*

THE GHOST at the Olde Angel Inn is Captain Swayze, a local militiaman, who was either killed in action or else died of his wounds after hiding in the basement of the inn during the War of 1812. The Americans burned down the hotel to find him.

In the ground floor, English pub-style bar, townsfolk will tell you the tramp of soldiery can still be heard coming from the cellars. While you are quite welcome to pop down and see if there's anyone there, they'd rather not join you, thanks very much.

Several people have even seen the captain, complete with blue frock coat and white trousers wearing a wig. Séances held at the inn have confirmed the captain's presence. When a reenactment of the local battle between English (and Canadian) soldiers and their American opponents was performed in Niagara-on-the-Lake, a member of the inn's staff went down to the cellars afterward and returned upstairs to report that "one of them is still walking about down there." An immediate investigation of the cellars showed them to be quite empty.

Innkeepers Peter and Diane Ling take a prosaic view of their intangible guest and whether or not he exists. But when the Lings took over the inn, and Peter was sleeping there alone, he brought with him their favorite lucky horseshoe. He was awakened by the sound of a loud crash and found the heavy iron horseshoe had been torn from the wall and hurled down in front of the front door. Perhaps the distinctly unlucky Captain Swayze didn't care for the good-luck charm.

When Peter Ling first heard the stories about Captain Swayze, he was silly enough to say laughingly, "I'd like to meet this ghost." Next day, an old newspaper with headlines detailing the ghostly goings-on appeared on the doorstep.

Perhaps that could be attributed to a human hand. Less easily explained is the evidence of tourism executive Duncan Ross, a provincial government official. Says Ross (and remember, his job is attracting visitors—many of them Americans—to Ontario), "Captain Swayze doesn't like Americans. If anyone goes into the inn with an American flag on his jacket, or anything like that identifying him as an American, glasses start falling off shelves."

All that trouble over the forty-ninth parallel almost two hundred years ago and things still aren't settled. At least, not down in the cellars of the Olde Angel Inn. But such "local difficulties" apart, the bar of the Olde Angel Inn is as pleasant and atmospheric a refreshment stop as any in Ontario.

OLDE ANGEL INN

Address:	224 Regent Street, Niagara-on-the-Lake, Box 1603, Ontario, Canada L0S 1J0
Telephone:	(905) 468-3411
Facilities:	English-style pub
Price Range:	Inexpensive to moderate

BANFF SPRINGS HOTEL

Banff, Alberta

THE MAGNIFICENT Banff Springs Hotel dominates the year-round resort of Banff, in the heart of Canada's Rocky Mountains. A massive 849-room property, it is modeled on a Scottish baronial castle. The guest rooms include sixty-eight suites and, although many of the furnishings are antiques, the standards of service are as efficient and up-to-date as can be found anywhere.

The setting is spectacular. That is, after all, one of the reasons the hotel was built here in the first place. But considering the property is now more than a hundred years old, its ancient facade hides the modern results of recent renovations.

Guests want for nothing. There are nineteen separate food and beverage outlets within the property, including specialty restaurants (try their oriental delicacies) and smart cocktail bars such as the Manor. This is a place to see and be seen.

Railroad pioneer Cornelius Van Horne masterminded the building of the Banff Springs, and its sister hotels across Canada, to encourage passengers to explore the countryside on the newly completed transcontinental Canadian Pacific Railway with a degree of comfort. The Banff Springs was opened in 1888 and quickly became one of the group's flagship properties. There are unforgettable views from every guest bedroom.

Since those days, the hotel has been carefully upgraded. It now includes a sauna and gymnasium, bowling alley, indoor miniature golf, a huge variety of meeting rooms, and a big new conference center and ballroom. Guests never need to leave: There are even fifty shops on site. But outdoors, the scenery and the sports facilities beckon, with golf, tennis, and horse-riding virtually on the spot, and some of Canada's top skiing on the nearby slopes. The Banff Springs Hotel, eighty-one miles from Calgary Airport, has literally become a hotel for all seasons.

THE GHOST at Banff Springs is Sam McAuley, a former bellman at the hotel. Before he died in 1969, McAuley always swore he would come back to the hotel after his death and help out when things got busy. He appears to have kept his promise. During the morning and evening rush hours, when guests are checking in and out, there is sometimes a delay before the present-day bellman answers a call and arrives at the guest's room. And when the bellman does arrive, he will occasionally be told, "It's okay, one of the other bellmen was here." When the guests are asked what the other bellman looked like, they invariably describe McAuley.

There are a trio of other ghost stories connected with the old property, and they can be learned during tours of the hotel. But Banff Springs is not always enthusiastic about admitting to its intangible guests.

"The value of a good ghost story is the way it's told," hotel spokesman Bob Warwick says. "These are friendly stories. We don't want to scare anyone."

BANFF SPRINGS HOTEL

> *Address:* P.O. Box 960, Banff, Alberta, Canada T0L 0C0
> *Telephone:* (403) 762-2211
> *Fax:* (403) 762-5755

Facilities:	Adjacent twenty-seven-hole championship golf course, alpine and Nordic skiing, extensive conference and meeting facilities, big choice of restaurants, twenty-four-hour room service
Price Range:	Moderate to expensive

OCEAN POINTE RESORT

Victoria, British Columbia

OCEAN POINTE RESORT is a new, luxurious property on Vancouver Island, overlooking Victoria's bustling Inner Harbor, an area now beautifully redeveloped to offer a host of leisure activities.

And Ocean Pointe Resort is at the hub of much fun. A family-run property, OPR—as it is familiarly known—has a very special, friendly, and intimate atmosphere that belies its size. With 250 guest rooms and suites and very extensive sporting and leisure facilities, it would be easy for guests to feel like just another body.

But Fred Stolle, wife Kathryn, and daughter Kristina have worked hard to establish a turn-of-the-century European ambiance and create that personal touch. Staff greet guests by name on arrival—and remember them.

There are two restaurants in the complex, the casual brasserie/deli-style Boardwalk and the elegant Victorian Restaurant; a piano bar; and many cozy nooks in the lobby lounge with its sweeping staircase.

But for rooms with a view, OPR must score among Canada's finest. The public rooms and almost all the guest accommodations have wide harbor views.

The pretty city of Victoria, with its English influences, is on the doorstep. Parks, gardens, rides in double-decker buses, harbor cruises, theaters, golf, water sports, and all the sights of the historic area are within easy reach.

OCEAN POINTE RESORT

THE GHOST of Ocean Pointe Resort is not exactly an apparition; it is more a spirit of place.

Ocean Pointe is built on an ancient Indian burial ground. When excavations were taking place as building started in 1992, bones, jewelry, and other ancient artifacts came to the surface.

Workmen began reporting feeling "strange" as they dug in this hallowed ground on Victoria's waterfront.

Rather than disturb the Indian spiritual influences further, the Stolle family, who had been overseeing work on their new hotel right from blueprint stage, decided to invite an Indian shaman to conduct pacifying rituals and calm the spirits of warriors long dead. Just to be on the safe side, they had a priest conduct an exorcism, too.

The result? A great sense of peace, says OPR's sales manager Kristina Stolle.

"But my parents and I were never worried by the Indian spirits," she says. "After all, we Stolles live quite happily just down the road in a haunted house."

But that is another story.

OCEAN POINTE RESORT

Address:	On the Harbor at 45 Songhees Road, Victoria, British Columbia, Canada V9A 6T3
Telephone:	(604) 360-2999
Fax:	(604) 360-1044
Facilities:	Health spa with indoor pool, sauna, racquetball, tennis, squash, rooms specially fitted for wheelchair use and the hearing-impaired
Price Range:	Expensive

TONQUIN INN

Jasper, Alberta

AT THE HEART of one of Canada's most attractive resort towns lies the smart new Tonquin Inn, a magnificent property ideal for family vacations.

There are 135 guest suites, carefully planned to suit every pocket. They range from luxury suites—some with balconies, fireplaces, and even saunas—to economy units with kitchenettes so visitors can do their own cooking. The rooms are bright, clean, and modern. Nonsmoking rooms are available on request. There is wheelchair accessibility.

Kitchenettes are handy, but it would be a pity to miss out on the Alberta prime rib served in the Tonquin Prime Rib Village Dining Room. Other refreshment stops include Nick's Bar and Lounge, and the licensed outdoor patio. The hotel has a luxurious indoor swimming pool and whirlpool, and there are also saunas and outdoor hot tubs for the hardy.

Jasper is in the center of the Jasper National Park, the largest and most beautiful park in the Canadian Rockies. The town itself is small and lends the feeling of being very close to nature. That is not surprising in a place where bears in the backyard are common.

Bears notwithstanding, this is a place for sampling the great outdoors. There are year-round activities for everyone. In summer, the

Rockies offer river rafting, mountain biking, cycling, fishing, horseback riding, hiking, tennis, and golf. In winter, choose from local heliskiing and cross-country skiing, to downhill skiing at Marmot Basin. And all year, there are plenty of wide open spaces to explore by car.

THE GHOST at the Tonquin Inn is an old railroad worker, who lodged there for years and is believed to have fallen from the caboose and disappeared after a drinking bout. Or is it? There is little doubt that both the Tonquin Inn and Jasper have a fascinating history, but one can't help feeling the stories have grown with each retelling.

The name *Tonquin*, for example.

"It was the name of an English ship," owner Karyn Decore explains. "They thought they could make it across Canada by river. They sailed up one of the rivers, but the ship was grounded. It was discovered by native Indians and everyone was killed."

Apparently, the Tonquin Valley took its name from the ill-fated ship, and the hotel likewise took its name from the valley. But one can't help wondering how a ship's crew, sailing inland from the Pacific, failed to notice a hazard blocking their route—the soaring, snowcapped Rocky Mountains.

Best not mention this to the Tonquin Inn's director of sales and marketing, Rick Bowie. It encourages him to tell tales that sound suspiciously like even greater flights of fancy.

"Some of the first people to stay in the hotel were railway workers," he says. "One stayed for two years. One night he had a few beers before going to work. He worked in the caboose and just disappeared."

Did he fall or was he pushed? More to the point, was his body found and buried beneath the hotel? Local opinion is divided on both issues.

"But," Bowie says, "we *could* have a ghost here."

Any evidence, apart from local gossip?

"Sometimes we still hear the mournful clanging of a railroad locomotive's bell," Bowie adds hopefully.

This is hardly surprising, since the railroad is right across the street from the inn. But even if the evidence of a ghost at the Tonquin Inn is distinctly thin, and unlikely to convince anyone except the most ardent psychic, the inn does deserve an entry in this book. It's a nice place to stay and the ghost stories might, just might, be true.

TONQUIN INN

Address: P.O. Box 658, Jasper, Alberta, Canada T0E 1E0
Telephone: (403) 852-4987, or for reservations (800) 661-1315
Fax: (403) 852-4413
Facilities: Resort property
Price Range: Moderate to expensive

HOTEL VANCOUVER

Vancouver, British Columbia

WHEN THE SOLIDLY traditional Hotel Vancouver was built in the late 1930s, it towered over surrounding edifices, its copper roof glistening in British Columbia's sunshine.

Today, that copper roof is a venerable green color, aged by the elements, but it graces what is still one of Vancouver's most handsome buildings. Its stone facade is decorated with sculptures in the massive, almost primitive style of the 1930s, yet the towers and gables and turrets are reminiscent of a French chateau.

That grandeur is typical of properties built for the Canadian Pacific Railway by its great visionary, William Cornelius Van Horne, in the 1800s. He set goals of almost unimaginable luxury in catering to the railroad's passengers, and this influence is still evident in the more modern of CP Hotel's properties. As a Canadian travel writer put it back in 1924, "These hotels are palatial and romantic resting places for travelers who desire relief . . . from the rush of modern business."

The Hotel Vancouver is no exception. Right in the heart of the city, the hotel's prewar, stylish atmosphere has been carefully preserved. Recently renovated, the property boasts marble and mirrors in profusion, period mahogany and maple furniture in the lobby, lounges, and guest rooms—even the bathrooms. Its cozy bars feature nightly entertainment, and there are two restaurants catering to a range of tastes and budgets. The health club's indoor pool reserves special space for a children's wading pool.

Vancouver's theaters, fine shops, and galleries are everywhere. Only a few minutes away is Robson Street with its specialist boutiques, bustling Chinatown, and the colorful Gastown district. And Stanley Park, 970 acres of formal gardens, peaceful walks, and pretty waterfalls, is only a short drive away. Vancouver's own ski area at St. Grouse Mountain is an added attraction.

THE GHOST at the Hotel Vancouver is an elegantly gowned guest of almost sixty years ago.

So many of the hotel's staff have seen her in sightings recorded back to the earliest days of the building welcoming visitors, that this lovely lady of the 1930s has been identified as a long-staying guest from 1939 to 1940.

Her name, sadly, is not recorded. But former elevator operators knew her well. She loved to ride up and down in the gilded elevator cabins, right up to the top floor of what was in her day the tallest building in Vancouver.

The present manager disclaims his intangible guest. But the lady obviously enjoys her weeks at the hotel and her rides in the elevator, for she has not checked out. Guests and staff alike are used to catching a glimpse of her slim figure in an otherwise empty elevator cabin. She is never seen getting out of it.

HOTEL VANCOUVER

Address:	900 West Georgia Street, Vancouver, British Columbia, Canada V6C 2W6
Telephone:	(604) 684-3131 or (800) 441-1414
Fax:	(604) 662-1929
Facilities:	Health club with indoor pool
Price range:	Expensive

SOME OTHER PHANTOMS

BESIDES THE properties detailed in the foregoing pages, there are a number of other North American hotels, inns, guesthouses, and bed-and-breakfasts believed to be haunted. In some cases, however, it was not possible to visit the accommodations, and in others it was not possible to ascertain details of the stories connected with the property.

Accommodations which fall into one or other of these categories are listed below in state alphabetical order.

The Williams House (Arkansas):
420 Quapaw Avenue, Hot Springs National Park, Arkansas 71901
(501) 624-4275

> Haunted by an unknown male who stomps around this bed-and-breakfast ringing bells, moving ornaments in a locked glass case and leaving behind the smell of cigarette smoke.

The Hyde Regency (California):
c/o The American Property Exchange
170 Page Street, San Francisco, California 94102
(415) 863-8484

> Short-term "catered housing" holiday facility. Haunted by an elderly bearded man who is often heard and sometimes seen by guests.

Cabbage Key (Florida):
P.O. Box 200, Pineland, Florida 33945
(813) 283-2278

> Laid-back island inn, restaurant, and bar where guests have reported "many unusual happenings" in one of the guest bedrooms, the kitchen, and the bar.

Bonnie Castle (Georgia):

2 Post Street, Grantville, Georgia 30220
(404) 583-2080

Turn-of-the-century bed-and-breakfast where, after a previous owner's death, there were reports of the air conditioning and lights switching themselves on and off while the electricity supply was disconnected.

Early Hill (Georgia):

1580 Lickskillet, Greensboro, Georgia 30642
(706) 453-7876

Bed-and-breakfast with two ghosts: a little girl and an old man who sits rocking on the porch.

The Haslam House (Georgia):

9489 Whitfield Ave., P.O. Box 49, Savannah, Georgia 31406
(800) 729-7787

The ghost is George, the original owner of the house, who is reputed to have been lynched after giving a poor performance in a minstrel show.

The Olivier House (Louisiana):

828 Toulouse, New Orleans, Louisiana 70122
(504) 525-8456

Atmospheric hotel, in the heart of the French Quarter, haunted by a young Confederate soldier and his sweetheart, who appear in the courtyard gardens, on the stairs, and in one of the guest bedrooms.

Copper Beech (Massachusetts):

Westwood, Massachusetts
(617) 449-5302
Write: Bed-and-Breakfast Associates, Bay Colony, P.O. Box 57166, Babson Park, Boston, Massachusetts 02157

Bed-and-breakfast reputedly haunted by the ghost of a runaway slave, mourning her lost child.

The Old Stagecoach Inn (Massachusetts):
P.O. Box 821, Groton, Massachusetts 01450
(508) 448-5614

The ghost is a man who appears in the dining room wearing a purple coat and a white wig in the style of the 1750s. Other ghosts from the same period have been reported.

The Victorian Villa Inn (Michigan):
601 N. Broadway, Union City, Michigan 49094
(517) 741-7383

Bed-and-breakfast haunted by Caroline, who died in 1910.

The Pollard (Montana):
2 North Broadway, Red Lodge, Montana 59068
(406) 446-0001 or 800-POLLARD

The ghost is a woman of the 1890s, seen walking on the top floor.

The Lodge at Cloudcroft (New Mexico):
P.O. Box 497, Cloudcroft, New Mexico 88317
(505) 682-2566

The ghost is a beautiful young maid, Rebecca, whose portrait hangs in the lounge. Murdered by her lumberjack lover in a fit of jealousy, she reputedly wanders the halls in search of a new romance with someone who won't mind her flirtatious ways.

The Reed House (North Carolina):
119 Dodge Street, Asheville, North Carolina 28803
(704) 274-1604

Haunted by a couple of invisible pool players.

Buxton Inn (Ohio):
313 E. Broadway, Granville, Ohio 43023
(614) 587-0001

No specter as such, just the sound of coins spilling on the floor when there is no one else around and no money to be seen.

Historic Shaniko Hotel (Oregon):
4th and E Street, Shaniko, Oregon
(503) 489-3341

Haunted by newlyweds murdered in their nuptial bed by hooligans.

The John Palmer House (Oregon):
4314 N. Mississippi Avenue, Portland, Oregon 97217
(503) 284-5893

The ghost is Lotta, an opera singer who lost her voice.

Admiral Farragut Inn (Rhode Island):
31 Clarke Street, Newport, Rhode Island 02840
(401) 848-8000

An inexplicable fresh breeze and a "presence" have both been reported in this hotel. A sick innkeeper was once handed a bottle of vitamin tablets by an unseen hand.

LaBorde House Inn (Texas):
601 E. Main, Rio Grande City, Texas 78582
(210) 487-5101

Historic old travelers' inn where lights turn themselves off and doors unlock without a key. Authentic period furnishings.

Raphael House (Texas):
500 W. Ennis Avenue, Ennis, Texas 75119
(214) 298-8586

The ghosts are Raymond and Julia, who apparently enjoy closing windows and slamming drawers upstairs in this bed-and-breakfast.

The Wiffletree Inn (Texas):
1001 N. Sycamore, Palestine, Texas 75801
(903) 723-6793

A "tastefully outrageous" (to quote the innkeepers) restored turn-of-the-century inn with a tidy-minded ghost who puts the vacuum cleaner back in the closet if it's left out after cleaning.

Edgewood Plantation (Virginia):

4800 John Tyler Hwy., Charles City, Virginia 23030
(804) 829-2982

> Bed-and-breakfast where the ghost of Lizzie, a former inhabitant, waits in vain for her lover to return from the Civil War.

Bluebeard's Castle Hotel (Virgin Islands):

P.O. Box 7480, Charlotte Amalie, St. Thomas, U.S. Virgin Islands 00801
(809) 774-1600, or for reservations (800) 524-6599

> Classy hotel closely connected with the legend of the pirate Bluebeard. He is believed to have turned the tower into a home for his bride, Mercedia Cordovan, whom he later saved from execution. Either, or both, may haunt the tower.

AUTHOR BIO

Robin Mead, a London resident and internationally known travel writer and author, has written twenty-six books and regularly contributes to more than fifty magazines and newspapers worldwide. A former chairman of the British Guild of Travel Writers, Mead is an elected fellow of the Royal Geographical Society in London. He also belongs to both of Britain's professional travel organizations: the Tourism Society, and the Institute of Travel and Tourism. *Haunted Hotels* is a North American sequel to *Weekend Haunts*, a guide to haunted hotels in Britain.